TOKYO

Exploring the City of the Shogun

To Brook Berlind
With great pleasure of
getting to know you

April 13th, 2009, Tokyo

Sumiko Enbutsu

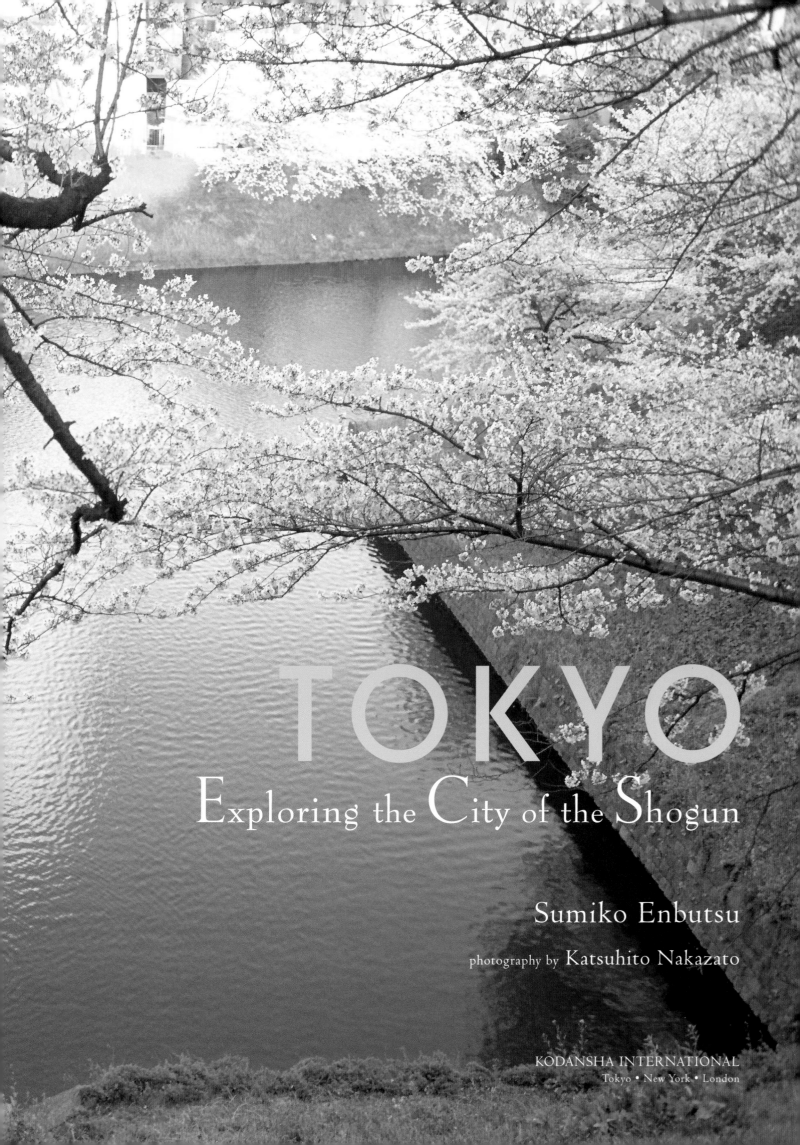

TOKYO
Exploring the City of the Shogun

Sumiko Enbutsu

photography by Katsuhito Nakazato

KODANSHA INTERNATIONAL
Tokyo • New York • London

NAMES: The names of some buildings, institutions, and landmarks alternately appear in the text and maps in the English or Japanese forms, the former for clarity's sake, the latter to assist in asking directions. Thus, the "Kasugano Sumo Stable" ("stable" being the term for a wrestler's team, dorm, and practice gym) will also be listed as "Kasugano-beya," the manner in which it is referred to by the Japanese. ● Japanese names of personages living and historical appear in the Japanese order, surname preceding given name. The author's and photographer's names appear in the Western order.

Distributed in the United States by Kodansha America, Inc., and in the United Kingdom and continental Europe by Kodansha Europe Ltd.

Published by Kodansha International Ltd., 17–14 Otowa 1-chome, Bunkyo-ku, Tokyo 112–8652, and Kodansha America, Inc.

First edition, 2007
15 14 13 12 11 10 09 08 07   10 9 8 7 6 5 4 3 2 1

Library of Congress Cataloging-in-Publication Data available online

www.kodansha-intl.com

LEGEND FOR MAPS

——	route of walk	鳥居	shrine
······	optional route	⊗⊗⊗	traffic light
●	point of interest/shop	⊗	school
卍	temple	❔ 🚇	subway exit

CAPTIONS

ABOVE: *Senjafuda*, Edo-style name cards left by donators and visitors to Fukagawa Shinmeigu shrine.

PAGE 1: Ote-mon Gate, site of the shogun's castle.

PAGE 2–3: Castle moat and cherry blossoms near the Imperial Palace at Chidorigafuchi (see map on page 10), long famous for its cherry blossoms.

PAGE 5 & ENDPAPERS: Map of Tokyo in the Edo Period (1600–1868).

Contents

Preface

Tokyo is an exciting modern city. Towering skyscrapers and sparkling neon lights attest to the city's astonishing vigor. Clean, efficient subways and bullet trains whisk passengers off to their desired destinations with unrivalled speed and reliability. Diverse gourmet restaurants serve the choicest seasonal delicacies to suit the palates of all. Entertainments and shops, offering dazzling arrays of the latest and the most quintessential Japanese fashions and gadgets and other goods, thrill the hearts of old and young alike.

Tokyo is an old city, too. The capital of Japan was founded by Shogun Tokugawa Ieyasu in 1603. First called Edo and renamed Tokyo in 1868, it has been Japan's center of government, business, and culture for over four hundred years. Even before the shogun came, valiant warriors had recognized this spot for its strategic importance in their operations since the 12th century. The city moreover is studded with archaeological sites offering evidence of prehistoric human habitation.

Tokyo is more than a single city; it comprises numerous villages and towns, each with a distinct character. But the city's rich and layered history is all too often concealed by incessant urban development, or, worse still, has been forever lost in the wake of various calamities and natural disasters.

Tokyo: Exploring the City of the Shogun invites non-Japanese-speaking residents and visitors to explore this complex mega-city on their own. The volume contains eight carefully selected walks with the main focus on the Edo built by Shogun Tokugawa Ieyasu. The introductory walk and the following five courses trace the city's early history. Asakusa, the area of the seventh walk, is older than Edo and was a more or less independent city until it was engulfed by Edo's sprawl in the early 19th century. Finally, Yanaka, the last walk, saw its growth boom after the 1868 Meiji Restoration and is a walker's haven today.

The book's detailed walking instructions, illustrated with accompanying maps, will allow the reader to safely navigate bustling main thoroughfares and unmarked backstreets. Lavish color photographs (and the occasional old painting and print) help evoke a sense of Tokyo's more human past. Any map of Tokyo's train and subway networks will be good companions to this book.

Barry Lancet and Michiko Uchiyama, editors at Kodansha International, created the book's basic concept. Katsuhito Nakazato contributed his excellent photographic skills in order to capture the nuances of life in Tokyo. Ann Ebrecht carefully tested all the walks firsthand and refined my descriptions. I express my deep gratitude to their valuable suggestions and enthusiastic cooperation with this project.

Sumiko Enbutsu
Tokyo

LEFT: A pond on the grounds of Atago-jinja shrine.
ABOVE: Gateway to the Kabukiza theater, a mainstay of Edo entertainment.

Introduction

City of the Shogun

THEN

In 1590, on the first day of the eighth month, Tokugawa Ieyasu, a senior veteran samurai who had survived many battles, arrived in Edo, then a seacoast hamlet at the head of Hibiya Cove. Not yet a shogun, he had been forced to move from his original fief in central Japan to this remote eastern region of Kanto by the order of his archrival and national ruler, Toyotomi Hideyoshi. Accompanied by a small retinue of trusted retainers, Ieyasu entered Edo Castle, his new home, at the edge of the Kojimachi Upland overlooking Edo Bay.

The "castle" he took over was little more than a cluster of dilapidated farmhouses encircled by mounds of earth. Ignoring his own comfort, he immediately began to develop a modest town below the hill, reclaiming the shallow sea and allocating land for housing and commerce. His city plan at this stage was a grid pattern modeled after the ancient city of Kyoto.

In 1598 Hideyoshi died. Winning the Battle of Sekigahara in 1600, Ieyasu seized power from Hideyoshi's young heir. Appointed shogun by the emperor in 1603, Ieyasu proclaimed Edo the new capital of Japan, taking Kyoto's place. He then redesigned his city, adopting a spiral plan connecting castle moats and rivers in a long chain of waterways reaching the Sumida River in the east and Edo Bay. He rebuilt the castle at its pivot, achieving a stunning grandeur. The luxurious residences of daimyo high lords surrounded the shogun's castle. Merchants and craftsmen were invited from all over the country to serve the needs of the military class's upper echelons.

Shogun, literally meaning "generalissimo," is an ancient title first accorded in the 8th century to a warrior leader on his expedition to conquer barbarians in northern Japan. As commander in chief of the entire samurai class, Shogun Ieyasu in 17th-century Japan stood at the top of the warrior government with the responsibility of keeping peace in the country. With authority to speak for the emperor on national affairs, Ieyasu promptly embarked on centralizing control over all military overlords (the daimyo) and their vassals, as well as on the construction of economic and social infrastructures. He unified the currency, standardized measurements, and re-laid the nationwide highway network branching out from Edo. Ieyasu resigned from office after two years, passing the scepter to his son, Hidetada, but retaining the real power for himself until his son was fit to rule. Hidetada reigned for eighteen years, to be succeeded by his son, Iemitsu. The hereditary right to the throne thus established and consolidated, the whole of Japan lay at the feet of the Tokugawa shoguns.

The Tatsumi Turret from the 17th century (*right*) and the restored Kikyo Gate (*left*) attest to the bygone splendor of the Tokugawa shoguns' Edo Castle.

CASTLE & PALACE GROUNDS

皇居東御苑 (江戸城本丸跡)

NEAREST STATION — JR Tokyo 東京, or Otemachi 大手町, various lines

ROUTE — Ote-mon gate 大手門 ➡ Sannomaru Shozokan Museum 三の丸尚蔵館 ➡ Hyakunin Bansho 百人番所 ➡ site of Edo Castle's inner citadel 江戸城本丸跡 ➡ site of castle tower 天守台跡
OPTION 1 Ninomaru Garden 二の丸庭園 ➡ Hirakawa-mon gate 平川門 ➡ Takebashi Station 竹橋駅
OPTION 2 Kita-Hanebashi-mon gate 北桔橋門 ➡ National Museum of Modern Art's Crafts Gallery 国立近代美術館工芸館 ➡ Takebashi Station 竹橋駅

ESTIMATED TIME — 30 minutes
ESTIMATED DISTANCE — 1 ¼ miles • 2 kilometers

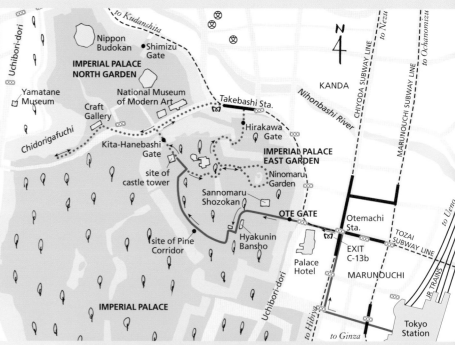

To maintain political stability, Japan closed its doors to foreign countries. The administrative patterns established by Ieyasu and his successors in the early decades of the 17th century remained basically unchanged until the middle of the 19th century. Peace and stability lead to remarkable growth in the national economy, which in turn encouraged the rise of a prosperous urban merchant class. Fast-growing communities of artisans, retailers, and laborers in big cities became a major source of demand economically and culturally. Many of the Edo-period arts, music, literature, and dramas, as represented by *ukiyo-e* woodblock prints and Kabuki, were created by and for urban commoners, and introduced new themes and styles befitting their new environment that differed from the established classic arts.

In Edo, the military class occupied about sixty percent of the city's space, and the commoners were herded into extremely crowded housing. To protect the reclaimed lowlands from floods, big rivers in the far north were diverted eastward by switching their upper and middle reaches away from Edo. Canals were built to bring fresh water from the Tama River to quench the thirst of Edo citizens and to irrigate the dry uplands for farming. Much of the city's growth thus hinged on these ambitious civil engineering projects outside Edo, the success of which Ieyasu was confident when he accepted his Edo assignment ordered by Hideyoshi. Though a conflagration in 1657 destroyed the first city of Edo, prompt reconstruction and expansion enabled the city to keep growing. By the turn of the 18th century, Edo supported a population of 800,000, then the largest city in the world.

By the time Commodore Perry arrived in 1853 to pry open Japan's doors to trade and diplomacy, the Tokugawa regime had lost its stamina. Eventually, the fifteenth shogun, Yoshinobu, returned his power to the emperor in what has become known as the Meiji Restoration of 1868, and the emperor moved to Edo Castle to spearhead Japan's modernization. In the city renamed Tokyo, spacious daimyo residences became factories and schools to absorb Western knowledge and technology. The basic city plan, however, changed little even after Tokyo was flattened twice in the 20th century—by the great Kanto earthquake in 1923 and by the air raids of the 1940s.

A Korean King's mission entering Edo Castle via the Ote Gate. Detail from screen (Edo-zu byobu), ca. 1640.

The city's historical overview thus given, we will set out on our explorations of the city beginning with the site of Edo Castle, now the Imperial Palace East Garden. (Open 9:00–16:30 March–October, 9:00–16:00 November–February; closed Mondays, Fridays, December 25–January 3, and special event days.)

We start at either JR Tokyo Station, taking one of the three Marunouchi exits, or the subway's Otemachi Station (Exit C-13b, the closest to the garden). If using Tokyo Station, follow the map to this subway exit. Head toward Ote-mon, the castle's front gate (*mon* means "gate") on the inner circle of moats. As you cross the broad Uchibori-dori toward the massive 17th-century castle walls, imagine seawater lapping at your feet. Hibiya Cove once reached this far until Ieyasu, becoming the shogun in 1603, launched his ambitious castle construction, filling in the cove with mud. The Imperial Palace is located off to your left, standing on the former western quarters of his expanded castle.

The Ote-mon, authentically restored in 1967 after its 1620 original was lost in the 1945 bombings, was used solely for the entry and exit by daimyo high lords, imperial envoys, and state guests. Arriving here, they were required to enter alone on foot, leaving their followers and carriages in a square where the Palace Hotel now stands. As each of about 270 lords came with an average retinue of 65 men, the hustle and bustle of crowds on the daimyo attendance day absolutely required good traffic control.

Inside the gate, you will be given a plastic chip, which you should return at the exit. On your right is Sannomaru Shozokan, the Museum of Imperial Collections, with a small gallery to display seasonally selected items. The gradually ascending path curves left to the large, flat wooden building of the Hyakunin Bansho guards' station. Pause to compare the stone walls around here and notice slight differences in the ways the stones are fitted together. The shogun divided the castle construction into portions, assigning each to rival lords, a policy that yielded fierce competition among the daimyo in the speed and perfection of their work.

Passing by the guards' station, continue to ascend until you come to a well-kept lawn, the site of Edo Castle's inner citadel. More the shogun's palace than a military fortress, a virtual "city" of tile-roofed buildings once stood here at about fifty-four feet (twenty meters) above sea level, commanding excellent views of the city below and Edo Bay beyond. The building complex consisted of three sections: the "front," an office staffed by elite samurai bureaucrats; the "middle back," the shogun's residence; and the "back quarters" for the harem, where his wife, concubines, their respective ladies-in-waiting, and maids all lived.

Upon arrival at the front, daimyo lords were required to deposit the larger of their two swords each customarily carried before proceeding to the rooms for meetings or important announcements.

A carpet of irises and azalea in Ninomaru Garden, with yellow water lilies floating in the pond.

Drawing a sword on the castle premises was strictly forbidden. A rare violation of the rule occurred in 1701. A young daimyo, Lord Asano, became enraged by what he perceived as callous and disdainful treatment from another daimyo, Lord Kira. Angered and frustrated, Asano rushed at Kira with the smaller sword he still retained as they passed in the Pine Corridor, a connecting hall so named from paintings of the tree on sliding screens. Asano was immediately sentenced to death for the breach, but Kira was held blameless. Hundreds of Asano's men became masterless, and forty-seven of his staunchly loyal retainers swore revenge upon their master's foe. This they did the following year, claiming the daimyo's head (see also the chapter on Ryogoku). The site of the incident is now a footpath in verdant woods to the left of the lawn.

At the lawn's far end stands a mound of granite blocks. Here a five-story tower once soared, the symbol of the Tokugawas' military supremacy. From here, choose between two options for your exit. One option is to go right from the tower base and bear left. You

RIGHT: The Shimizu Gate, the Imperial Palace North Garden.

BOTTOM: The double-arched span of the Nijubashi bridge crosses a moat bordering the public Imperial Plaza in the foreground and the Imperial Palace in the background, with the Fushimi Turret glimpsed in the distance.

will descend a short hill and can then exit via the Hirakawa-mon to the left. But it would be a pity to miss the lovely Ninomaru Garden (directly before you as you descend), originally landscaped by the famous samurai gardener Kobori Enshu (1579–1647) and restored in 1968. Sheltered in deep woods and moats from the hectic business districts outside, the classic stroll garden is a haven in the heart of Tokyo. It is especially beautiful in April through May when cherry blossoms, azaleas, and irises bloom in abundance.

A second option is to go around the tower base to use the Kita-Hanebashi-mon for a spectacular view of the perpendicular stone walls rising from the deep moats. After exiting the garden, you may go right to reach Takebashi Station on the Tozai Line. If, however, you take the pedestrian overpass immediately on the left, it links the former northern enclosure of the castle, now the Imperial Palace North Garden, with the wonderful Crafts Gallery of the National Museum of Modern Art.

LEFT: The stone foundation of a once-grand castle tower.

Nihonbashi & Ningyocho

The Heart of the Old City

日本橋　人形町

小網町

Wooden Nihonbashi bridge and the Nihonbashi-gawa, the hub of commodity shipping and pedestrian traffic of old Edo. Detail from screen (Edo-zu byobu), ca. 1640.

THEN

Nihonbashi—"Bridge of Japan"—was the nation's most famous and important bridge during the Edo period (1600–1868). Designated by Shogun Tokugawa Ieyasu in 1603 as the hub of the nationwide highway network, the wooden structure's sixteen-foot (five-meter) span became both a destination and departure point for journeys to and from the new capital city. In those days, when travel routes doubled as "information highways" constantly traversed by messengers, news of all kinds arrived and spread from Nihonbashi.

The river under the bridge, the Nihonbashi-gawa, became the artery of the city's commerce. Wealthy merchants from Kyoto and Osaka opened their branches along the river to capitalize on Edo's booming economy. In time the riverside became the site of sophisticated business transactions. Meanwhile, steady employment in the fast-growing city attracted craftsmen and laborers from surrounding provinces, and entertainers of all genres rushed to delight their ever-appreciative audiences.

A fish market opened on the bridge's northeastern end, initially to supply the large kitchen of Edo Castle. Later, with the shogun's permission, fishmongers sold the remains of the official purveyance to the public. As the daily fresh catches from Edo Bay were so bountiful, the market grew rapidly, becoming one of the three biggest money-making centers of Edo, along with the Kabukiza theater and the Yoshiwara red-light district. High-spirited fishmongers with handsome demeanors and sharp speech were admired as the ideal of Edokko—the townspeople of Edo.

Near the bridge, Mitsui Takatoshi (1622–94), an ex-samurai from Ise Province (now Mie Prefecture), opened the Edo branch of his Kyoto-based Echigoya kimono store in 1673, thereby laying the foundations of the Mitsui *zaibatsu* financial and industrial conglomerate and what was to become Mitsukoshi Department Store. Mitsui achieved great success retailing kimono materials for cash. His store also offered a speedy sewing service that earned the praise of up-and-coming customers in the burgeoning city, who could not afford to have a large wardrobe at home but needed to be dressed properly for important occasions. Using his characteristic political savvy and strong management skills, Mitsui also maintained business with the ruling class, especially with the shogun's harem, where demand was high for luxurious brocade and handcrafted silk.

With the advent of railroads in the Meiji period (1868–1912), inland shipping declined, but Nihonbashi remained the proud symbol

of modern Tokyo, its old wooden bridge replaced by a beautiful granite structure completed in 1911. The bridge retained its pivotal importance, designated as Point Zero from which to measure the distances of all Japan's trunk highways. The fish market continued to enjoy brisk business, and Mitsui's kimono store became a modern department store. After the great Kanto earthquake in 1923, Nihonbashi's status began to decline in the wake of the fish market's move to Tsukiji. Increasing Western imports forced the area's traditional businesses to close down. A flurry of post–World War II reconstruction in the devastated city caused the beautiful and symbolic bridge to fall under the shadow of roaring traffic on an overhead highway—a humiliating plight yet to be remedied.

The walk traces Nihonbashi's development and extends to Ningyocho, a charming town that sprang from the Kabuki theater district. Both the Kabuki and Yoshiwara districts were integral parts of the famous bridge's neighborhoods. While the brothels were moved early in 1656 to the city's northern periphery, the bustling, dense cluster of Kabuki and puppet theaters stayed on through most of the Edo period until they finally moved north in 1841 to Asakusa. Puppet craftsmen, however, preferred to remain in their home ground, giving the deserted town a new name—Ningyocho, or "puppet town."

TOP TO BOTTOM: An old abacus used by Edo-period shop clerks, the Ozu Collection; Edo *Shopping Guide*, 1824, the Ozu Collection; handmade brushes, Yubendo.

CLOCKWISE FROM TOP LEFT: Tasteful curtain for the shop front of Yubendo, purveyor of classic stationery and artist supplies; arrays of pigment jars for traditional Nihonga painting, Yubendo; colorful pallet of handmade Japanese paper (*washi*), Ozu; nostalgic Yamatoya, specializing in the old-fashioned *katsuo-bushi* business.

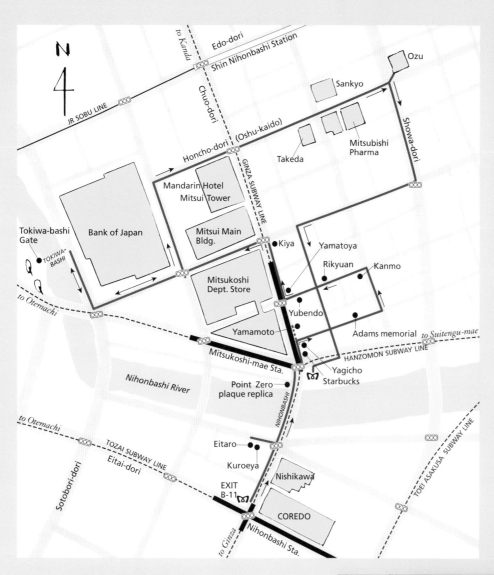

PART 1 NIHONBASHI 日本橋

NEAREST STATION Nihonbashi 日本橋 on the Ginza Subway Line 銀座線 or Tozai Subway Line 東西線

ROUTE Nishikawa textiles 西川 ➡ Kuroeya lacquerware 黒江屋 ➡ Eitaro sweets 栄太郎 ➡ Nihonbashi bridge 日本橋 ➡ Yagicho *katsuo-bushi* fish flakes 八木長 ➡ Yamamoto seaweed 山本 ➡ William Adams Memorial 三浦按針屋敷跡 ➡ Kanmo fish paste shop 神茂 ➡ Rikyuan *soba* noodles 利久庵 ➡ Yubendo stationery 有便堂 ➡ Yamatoya *katsuo-bushi* 大和屋 ➡ Kiya cutlery 木屋 ➡ Mitsui Main Building 三井本館 and Mitsukoshi Department Store 三越 ➡ Bank of Japan 日本銀行 ➡ Tokiwa-bashi Gate 常盤橋 門 ➡ (Honcho-dori) ➡ Ozu paper shop 小津和紙 ➡ Mitsukoshi-mae Subway Station 三越前駅 ➡ Part 2

ESTIMATED TIME 40 minutes

ESTIMATED DISTANCE 2 miles • 3.2 kilometers

NOW

Begin your walk at Nihonbashi Station, ideally arriving on the Ginza or Tozai Line. Avoid Sundays and holidays as many shops are closed.

Leaving Nihonbashi Station via Exit B-11, emerge on Chuo-dori, or the old Tokaido Road, and turn left to reach the landmark bridge visible straight ahead. Of the many textile shops that used to line this street, advancing from Kyoto and Osaka to 17th-century Edo, only Nishikawa remains in business, now dealing in apparel and bedding. On the left-hand street just before the bridge, Kuroeya (second building, second floor) has dealt in fine lacquerware since the turn of the 18th century. Next door, Japanese confectioner Eitaro has evolved from a peddler of sweet dumplings favored by busy fish-market workers. Its quiet restaurant is recommended for sampling traditional cakes with green tea, or the reasonably priced, tasty set menu lunches (closed on Sundays and holidays).

Back on the route, notice a round plaque at the bridge's center marking Point Zero—the hub of Japan's highways. A replica for easy viewing is placed at the bridge's far end, along with a stone inscribed with distances to major Japanese cities. Kyoto, it tells us, is 315 miles (503 kilometers) from this point.

Crossing the intersection toward Starbucks, you will enter the site of the old fish market, which once occupied several large blocks on the east side of Chuo-dori. Although the market has moved to Tsukiji, many dealers in seafood products have remained, a large number of them specializing in *katsuo-bushi*, a basic Japanese culinary ingredient made of steamed, fermented, and dried bonito fillets. *Katsuo-bushi* was treasured by samurai as an auspicious gift because of a pun on the words connoting "victorious (*katsu*) warrior (*bushi*)." To the left of Starbucks, find Yagicho, *katsuo-bushi* dealer since 1737, now also promoting other traditional cooking items. Passing a few buildings farther ahead on Chuo-dori you will find Yamamoto Nori, specializing in the dark green seaweed indispensable to sushi rolls.

Turning right at Yagicho, walk straight, looking for a stone monument squeezed between shops in the second left-hand block. The inconspicuous stone commemorates Miura Anjin, or William Adams (1564–1620), a British sailor on board a Dutch ship, the *Liefde*, which reached southern Japan in 1600. His adventurous life inspired James Clavell's best-selling novel, *Shogun*, in 1975.

Past the Adams memorial, turn left and take the second small street left around the Kanmo fish paste shop. With showcases that are more reminiscent of a confectioner's, the shop, founded in 1688, is one of the oldest in this area.

TOP: The granite Nihonbashi bridge regains its classic elegance in the evening.

BOTTOM LEFT: An ornate streetlamp of Nihonbashi bridge.

BOTTOM RIGHT: The Bank of Japan (*left*), 1896, and the Mitsui Main Building (*right*), 1929, both Important Cultural Properties of Japan, with the Mitsui Tower, 2005, in the back.

As you head back to Chuo-dori, you will find a good soba noodle restaurant on the right, called Rikyuan, with a classic shop front using a bamboo screen. (Open 11:00–20:30 Mondays through Fridays, 11:00–16:00 on Saturdays; closed Sundays and holidays.) Closer to Chuo-dori, Yubendo on the left is a traditional stationery store with a faithful base of customers among artists and calligraphers. A whole spectrum of pigments for Japanese painting is on display on shelves, and handcrafted calligraphy brushes are favored for their smooth touch on paper. Across the street from Yubendo, Yamatoya lies in a nostalgic building and, in the same tradition as nearby Yagicho, keeps an old-fashioned *katsuo-bushi* business.

Turn right on Chuo-dori to visit Kiya, a corner cutlery shop founded in 1792. Connoisseurs shop at this well-stocked store to choose from an array of traditional and imported knives and scissors, including gardening and ikebana scissors made using time-honored forging techniques of swordsmiths, or the Danjuro brand kitchen knives featuring high-tech steel for the cutting edges.

To explore the west side of Chuo-dori, cross over to Mitsukoshi Department Store and walk straight along its right-hand side, admiring on your right the classical Mitsui Main Building with fluted columns. This street, the cradle of the Mitsui financial and industrial conglomerate, was once lined with rows of tile-roofed, wooden buildings all sporting the same Mitsui logo as depicted by Edo woodblock-print artists Hiroshige and Hokusai.

In the next block at the end of the street, the classical Bank of Japan building is a fine example of the modified Renaissance-style architecture typical of the Meiji period (1868–1912). The central bank stands where the shogun first located his gold mint in 1601. Beyond it, off to the right of the traffic light and just up the block, a small stone bridge underneath the expressway leads to the site of the Tokiwa-bashi Gate of Edo Castle. While the Ote-mon gate, 900 yards (800 meters) to the west, was for official use by the shogun and dignitaries (see the Introduction), the Tokiwa-bashi Gate was a service entrance interfacing between the castle premises and the commercial towns. The stone-walled gate helps conjure images of licensed merchants like Mitsui clearing guard inspection to enter the castle center.

When the future shogun arrived in 1590, this whole area was a vast swamp traversed by the Hirakawa river, now a stagnant stream renamed the Nihonbashi-gawa and overshadowed by a huge expressway, and the site of Tokiwa Gate was the landing for boatmen. An ancient trail ran northeast from here through reedy marshes to reach Asakusa and northern Japan. The trail, incorporated in Ieyasu's initial town plan, was renamed Honcho.

A notable concentration of pharmaceutical companies on Honcho-dori two blocks beyond Chuo-dori is another vestige of Ieyasu's early development. He allocated this section initially as a first-aid station for workers in the construction of Edo Castle. These eventually evolved into modern pharmaceutical companies, including Takeda, Sankyo, and Mitsubishi Pharma.

Where Honcho-dori is intercepted by Showa-dori (with an expressway overhead), look to the other side of the highway to find the dark gray building of the Ozu paper shop, "wrapped" with a slatted wooden decoration. Based there since 1653, Ozu offers a wide range of *washi* handcrafted paper from historic papermaking villages all over Japan, as well as selections of calligraphy utensils and paper crafts.

Leaving Ozu, go left and turn right at the next traffic light to return to Nihonbashi bridge. For the extended walk to Ningyocho, take the Hanzomon Line to Suitengu-mae Station, one stop. Using Exit 5 of the station, make a U-turn right to visit Suitengu shrine. Expecting mothers often come here to pray for safe births and revisit to give thanks after birth. Fairs on the 5th, 15th, and 25th of the month, as well as the main festival on May 5, Children's Day, are good occasions to share in the festivities.

Backtracking to the major intersection, walk straight along the left side of Ningyocho-dori to find Dai-Kannon-ji temple up some steps set back from the main street. Nearby is an evocative lane lined with old wooden buildings and numerous potted plants, leaving just enough space for a visitor to walk. The stretch of traditional restaurants and drinking houses extends to the next block.

Opposite Dai-Kannon-ji, the Hiyama quality beef shop offers savory sukiyaki in old-fashioned *tatami*-mat rooms upstairs. (Open 11:30–14:00, 17:00–21:00; closed Sundays and holidays.) Backtracking to the Hibiya Line subway entrance, turn left to enter Amazake Yokocho, an exciting shopping street. Among the numerous shops and diverse businesses, Iwaido specializes in *tsuzura* (boxlike lacquered storage baskets) with a family crest on each. These are made to order for sumo wrestlers and traditional performing artists. From nearby Bachiei *shamisen* shop, you might hear the strumming of *shamisen*—traditional three-stringed instruments.

ABOVE: Old-fashioned Kikuya restaurant comes to life in the evening, near Dai-Kannon-ji.

FACING PAGE, TOP: Suitengu shrine associated with water, hence, the birth of babies.

FACING PAGE, BOTTOM: A votive wooden plaque (*ema*), hung at Suitengu, with the design of an Edo-style firemen's standard.

PART 2 NINGYOCHO 人形町

NEAREST STATION   Suitengu-mae 水天宮前 on the Hanzomon Subway Line 半蔵門線

ROUTE   Suitengu shrine 水天宮 ➡ Dai-Kannon-ji 大観音寺 ➡ Amazake Yokocho shopping street 甘酒横丁 ➡ Iwaido storage baskets 岩井堂 ➡ Bachiei *shamisen* shop ばち英 ➡ Ningyocho Station 人形町駅

ESTIMATED TIME   20 minutes

ESTIMATED DISTANCE   about ½ mile • 800 meters

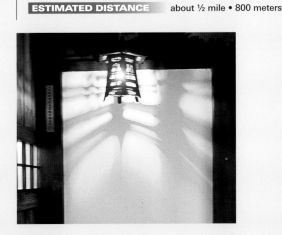

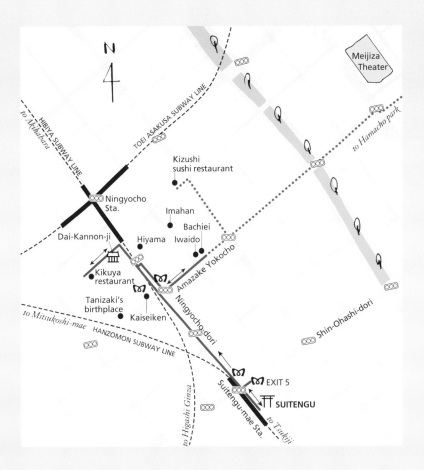

Ryogoku & Asakusa-bashi

The Sumo Quarters and Environs

THEN

During Edo times, the summer began with fireworks over the Sumida on the evening of May 28 in the old lunar calendar. The venue was the river's banks near Ryogoku-bashi, the first bridge built across the river in 1660. Large open spaces on both ends accommodated entertainers who were allowed to put up all kinds of shows and games for three months beginning with the pyrotechnic display. Anxious for the thrilling entertainment season's grand launch, the poor flocked to the riversides, while the rich caroused on *yakatabune* pleasure boats. Restaurants set up verandas for festival-goers to wine and dine while enjoying the cool breeze.

There was no bridge spanning the Sumida in Shogun Tokugawa Ieyasu's first city plan because he considered the big river the eastern defense line to block an enemy attack. However, after Ieyasu's death, when the fire of 1657 devoured the city, many people died at the river's edge, unable to flee any farther. That tragedy, as well as the need to relieve urban congestion, prompted the shogunate to build Ryogoku-bashi at the river's junction with the Oshu-kaido highway. With more bridges constructed later upstream and downstream, these links expedited the city's expansion east and south. O-Edo, or Great Edo, the expanding metropolis, thus flourished from what had originally been Ieyasu's compact city.

The Ryogoku-bashi neighborhoods were kept clear of buildings to create a firebreak, but Edo's newfound entrepreneurs obtained licenses for using the spaces on the condition that they do so in summertime only. A bustling village of makeshift sheds mushroomed on the riversides, resembling a many-ringed circus.

LEFT: Ephemeral flowers of fire fizzling in the night sky.

RIGHT: *Yakatabune* pleasure boats sallying forth under a fireworks display.

23

RYOGOKU & ASAKUSA-BASHI
両国－浅草橋

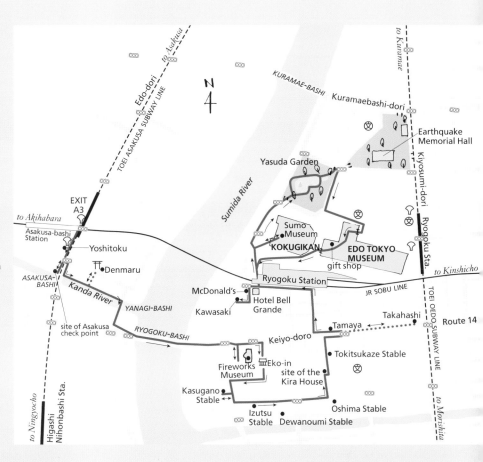

NEAREST STATION　Asakusa-bashi 浅草橋 on JR
Sobu Line or Toei Asakusa Subway Line 都営浅草線

ROUTE　Yoshitoku toy shop 吉徳 ➡
Asakusa-bashi bridge 浅草橋 ➡ Yanagi-bashi bridge 柳橋 ➡
Ryogoku-bashi bridge 両国橋 ➡ Fireworks Museum 花火
史料館 ➡ Eko-in temple 回向院 ➡ Kasugano Sumo Stable
春日野部屋 ➡ Izutsu Stable 井筒部屋 ➡ Oshima Stable 大島
部屋 ➡ site of Kira House 吉良邸跡 ➡ Tokitsukaze Stable
時津風部屋 ➡ Tamaya noodle restaurant 玉屋 ➡ JR Ryogoku
Station 両国駅 ➡ Kokugikan Sumo Stadium 国技館 ➡ Yasuda
Garden 安田庭園 ➡ Edo Tokyo Museum 江戸東京博物館 ➡
JR Ryogoku Station 両国駅 ➡ Kawasaki *chanko* restaurant
ちゃんこ川崎

ESTIMATED TIME　50 minutes

ESTIMATED DISTANCE　2 ¼ miles • 3.5 kilometers

TOP: A Sumida cruise boat on the day's last run at sunset.

BOTTOM LEFT: The Asahi Beer Building, designed to suggest a mug filled with sparkling amber beer.

BOTTOM, CENTER: Pleasure boats moored on the Kanda river with the arched green Yanagi-bashi bridge in the background.

BOTTOM RIGHT: An elegantly coiffured and costumed *hina* doll from Yoshitoku.

Meanwhile, on the east side of Ryogoku-bashi, Eko-in was built for the souls of victims in the 1657 fire. To defray the maintenance costs, the temple was authorized in 1766 to host sumo tournaments. Later it became the only licensee of the biannual tournament.

Today, the fireworks show is held in July farther upstream on the Sumida. Sumo, now based at the modern Kokugikan Stadium, continues to be Ryogoku's most treasured asset.

NOW

Our exploration starts at Asakusa-bashi on the bridge's west side. Using Asakusa-bashi Station on the JR Sobu Line or subway Toei Asakusa Line, leave by the East Exit if arriving by the JR line, or Exit A3 if by subway.

Turning right from the station exit, you will soon come to Asakusa-bashi bridge, where the Oshu-kaido highway crosses the Kanda River, reaching out from a highrise jungle beyond the bridge. The river, flowing into the Sumida off to your left, formed the northern stretch of the spiraling castle moat chain. An important checkpoint once stood here where guards would scrutinize travelers and boats to root out any criminals or illegal cargo. The site is marked by a low square stone pillar among bushes by the bridge. Local businesses in nearby neighborhoods would capitalize on travelers who had been held for long periods at the gate and sell souvenirs to them. Among the many doll and toy shops still in business, Yoshitoku, established in 1711, is the oldest and most reputable according to contemporary residents in and around Tokyo.

Backtracking from the bridge toward Yoshitoku, cross Edo-dori at the traffic light and bear right to walk along the Kanda. Beyond many boathouses projecting over the waters, note an old-fashioned green bridge, Yanagi-bashi, or "Willow Bridge," so named after the water-loving tree often planted along riversides.

Cross Yanagi-bashi and walk straight. Where traffic converges from many directions is a broad junction, originally an open clearing for fire prevention exploited by Edo townspeople for summertime entertainment. Turn left to walk over Ryogoku-bashi, rebuilt in 1932.

The view from the bridge is wonderful despite the annoying traffic. Close to the Sumida's estuary, the river runs slowly, gently rocking sea gulls afloat on the water. A few extra *yakatabune* pleasure boats may be rolling on the surging waves at the junction of the Kanda, preparing for an evening cruise, paper lanterns lit.

Walk straight across Ryogoku-bashi, turn right at the second traffic light to cross Keiyo-doro, and go left to visit Eko-in temple, marked by a modern chestnut-brown gate.

Just before the temple, you can make a brief stop at the Hanabi Shiryokan (Fireworks Museum) to see a small collection of *hanabi*-related memorabilia. The gallery is in the rear of the black-and-gray Sumitomo Fudosan high-rise, behind restaurant Le Parc. See rocket

A head-on clash of sumo wrestlers, settled in seconds.

fireworks made in perfect spherical form to produce maximum combustion—a relatively small 1½-inch-diameter (4.2 centimeters) ball creates a burst 165 yards (150 meters) across! You can also enjoy a thirteen-minute film on the making of fireworks. (Open 12 NOON–16:00, Fridays through Sundays, and daily in August.)

Inside Eko-in's gate, the bamboo-lined approach to the sleek, modern main hall gives a gentle and pleasing impression. A large natural stone on the left, carved with two *kanji* representing "power" (力) and "memorial" (塚), marks a sumo sanctuary dedicated to retired or deceased great wrestlers.

The temple was home to the first permanent sumo stadium named Kokugikan (the Hall of National Sport). Built in 1909 by Dr. Tatsuno Kingo, the chief architect of Tokyo Station and the Bank of Japan, the beautiful domed brick building was honored with frequent visits by emperors, imperial princes, and state guests until it was badly damaged by a heavy air raid on March 9, 1945.

Opposite the pet cemetery in the left-hand compound, which is one of the more recognizable parts of the temple, stand numerous old stone monuments dedicated to the victims of shipwrecks, fires, and other disasters subsequent to the 1657 fire, some with interesting bas-reliefs demonstrating fine masonry.

Exiting from the small rear gate, turn right and then left, soon finding the Kasugano-beya sumo stable in the right-hand block, housed in an eight-story modern building with an entrance resembling a shrine roof. Almost all sumo stables have both training rings and dormitories for young wrestlers in the same building. Notice a vertical wooden plate by the door, inscribed with the stable name in *kanji* characters. Based here since 1925, when retired *yokozuna* Tochigiyama founded it, Kasugano-beya is one of the most successful stables in sumo. It has produced two *yokozuna* (the most prestigious rank attainable) during its eighty-plus-year history—a considerable achievement given that only about one out of every four hundred freshmen attain that rank.

Retrace your steps and after turning right and immediately left, you will see the Izutsu-beya, a small milky white building with a nameplate. If you see many bicycles parked in front, it means that wrestlers are inside training. Off to the right of the next traffic light is another stable, Dewanoumi-beya, the head stable of the Dewanoumi group. Farther ahead on the main street, a square plate above eye level with an orange-colored handprint marks Oshima-beya.

Turning left just before the Oshima Stable, you come to a T-junction where beautifully plastered white walls encircle the site of Lord Kira's house. Lord Kira, the object of the forty-seven samurais' revenge (see the Introduction), is immortalized in the Kabuki and Bunraku plays *Chushingura*. Despite being portrayed as a wicked foe in the dramas, Lord Kira was, according to some scholars, actually highly esteemed by his people. When the large Kira estate here was being carved up for modern development, neighbors raised funds from their own pockets to buy a fraction of the land around a garden well where, it is said, the vengeful samurai washed Kira's severed head. They donated the property to the local municipality for a park. A memorial service is held every year on the weekend closest to December 14, the day the revenge was carried out.

Leaving the Kira site, turn left twice, passing by still another sumo stable, Tokitsukaze-beya, in the right-hand middle block. Back

TOP: Colorful banners with wrestlers' names, gifts from fans.

BOTTOM LEFT: *Chanko*, the hearty everyday meal for sumo wrestlers, served to gourmet customers of Kawasaki restaurant.

BOTTOM RIGHT: Off-duty junior wrestlers on a street near Ryogoku Station.

at Route 14, cross the highway at the nearby traffic light. Before turning left to visit the new Kokugikan, you might like a stopover at Takahashi, a shop selling sumo-themed souvenirs in the second right-hand block. Otherwise, go left, passing by the Tamaya soba noodle restaurant almost immediately on the right—a good place for a light meal. In the cozy restaurant, young wrestlers often share tables with local customers.

Take the next right, go left along the JR Ryogoku Station, and turn right at its end. You will have no trouble recognizing the sumo stadium ahead.

An architectural fusion of traditional designs and modern construction expertise, the new Kokugikan, completed in 1984, hosts sumo matches for only forty-five days a year, in three tournaments in January, May, and September. The big hall is therefore designed to be converted from sumo to other purposes with relative ease. Also a fine example of ecological recycling systems, the beautiful large green roof harvests rainwater and solar energy. The rainwater fills 70 percent of a 3,000-cubic-ton tank, providing water for stadium use.

Enter the attached Sumo Museum through the first gate on your right. Open to the public on days when there is no tournament, the exhibits are part of a large collection of trophies, old costumes, woodblock prints, photographs, and other memorabilia, and are frequently changed. (Open 9:30–16:30; closed Saturdays, Sundays, national holidays, and New Year.)

North of the Kokugikan, the Yasuda Garden features a lovely pond whose water level varies from time to time to produce different impressions. Landscaped at the turn of the 18th century for Lord Honjo of the Kasama Domain (now part of Ibaraki Prefecture), the traditional garden is one of Japan's famous so-called daimyo gardens. It features a restored tidal pond, whose construction employs a technique unique to Edo-style landscaping developed along the Sumida River. The water, which previously used to rise and fall with the ebb and flow of Edo Bay's tides, is now controlled mechanically, using a large underground tank. The rock formations and a brightly painted red bridge add to the garden's scenic beauty. In the wake of the Meiji Restoration, Yasuda Zenjiro (1838–1921), financier and founder of the Yasuda *zaibatsu*, acquired the garden, and later donated it to Tokyo; hence the garden name in his memory.

Exit from the garden's other end and turn right, glancing at the tower of the Earthquake Memorial Hall designed by Ito Chuta, the architect of Tsukiji Hongan-ji temple (see the Tsukiji walk), visible above the trees straight ahead. When you see the sumo stadium, turn left and then bear right to cut across the parking area toward a stained-glass-walled restaurant. Beyond the restaurant door is the entrance to the shopping area of Edo Tokyo Museum. Follow the signs inside to the museum shop teeming with gift items.

Exiting from the nearby glass doors, bear left to reach the JR station. If you are interested in *chanko*, a kind of stew eaten by sumo wrestlers as their staple food, try Kawasaki, following the map to find it. As you near the modest restaurant down a small alley directly across from the Hotel Bell Grande, the unmistakable smell of chicken broth grows irresistible. Opened in 1937 by retired wrestler Yokoteyama, Kawasaki pioneered serving authentic *chanko* to the public. (Open 17:00–22:00, or until the food is sold out; closed Sundays and holidays. Tel: 3631–2529.)

Fukagawa

In the Footsteps of the Haiku Poet Basho

The summer festival of Tomioka Hachimangu shrine: a golden portable shrine (*mikoshi*) lifted high by local residents as they are doused with water.

THEN

In 1596, shortly after Tokugawa Ieyasu set about developing the Nihonbashi area, he went hunting on horseback across the Sumida River. His destination on the river's east side was a vast marshland, through which a straight canal called the Onagi-gawa reached Gyotoku, now part of Chiba Prefecture.

While chasing game among overgrown reeds, Ieyasu found several workers cutting ditches to drain the wetland. Stopping his horse, he asked them the area's name. Their leader replied, "It has no name, sir, because this swampland has no village yet." Ieyasu then inquired, "Who are you and what is your name?" "I am Fukagawa Hachiroemon from Settsu Province (now part of Osaka Prefecture), and these are my followers," came the reply. "Well, then, name it Fukagawa," said Ieyasu. With the future shogun's sanction on his private land development, Hachiroemon established his village on the unmapped Sumida wilderness.

After the Edo fire of 1657 destroyed much of the city, southern Fukagawa boomed with official developments as major commodity markets relocated from the congested city center. Subsequent to the construction of Ryogoku-bashi (see Ryogoku), Eitai-bashi bridge was built in 1698 to facilitate pedestrian traffic from Nihonbashi to Fukagawa. The waterborne transportation systems became highly developed, too, using the Onagi-gawa as a channel connecting the Pacific Coast and the Sumida. Brisk business attracted enterprising merchants in lumber and rice—two necessities for life in Edo. Among the legendary lumber merchants, Kinokuniya Bunzaemon is famous for a fabulous fortune he amassed during the construction of Edo Castle, and equally infamous for squandering it all and ultimately dying in poverty.

The area's booming economy stimulated the growth of teahouses around Tomioka Hachimangu, initially a modest shrine where local sailors worshipped. Offering all kinds of services—more than just a cup of tea—to the rough-tempered, free-spending mariners, the refreshment stands eventually became a large red-light district to rival in fame and prosperity the Yoshiwara licensed quarters in Asakusa.

A distance away from the vibrant southern business districts, northern Fukagawa was still a rustic and idyllic area when the poet Matsuo Basho (1644–94) moved from Nihonbashi to Fukagawa in 1680. The poet became so enamored with an exotic banana tree, or *basho*, planted under the eaves of his modest abode that he changed his pen name, Tosei ("Green Peach"), to Basho. In 1689, he set off on a five-month

FUKAGAWA 深川

NEAREST STATION Monzen Nakacho 門前仲町 on the Tozai Subway Line 東西線 or Toei Oedo Subway Line 都営大江戸線

ROUTE Fukagawa Fudo temple 深川不動 ➡ Tomioka Hachimangu shrine 富岡八幡宮 ➡ Kisaragi-bashi bridge 木更木橋 ➡ Fukagawa Edo Museum 深川江戸史料館 ➡ Kiyosumi Garden 清澄庭園 ➡ Mannen-bashi bridge 萬年橋 ➡ Statue of Basho ➡ Basho Memorial Museum 芭蕉記念館 ➡ Fukagawa Shinmeigu shrine 深川神明宮

OPTION 1 Iseki *dojo* restaurant 伊世喜 ➡ Kiyosumi Shirakawa Station 清澄白河駅
OPTION 2 Kyokin *soba* noodle restaurant 京金 ➡ Morishita Station 森下駅

ESTIMATED TIME 70 minutes
ESTIMATED DISTANCE 3 miles • 5 kilometers

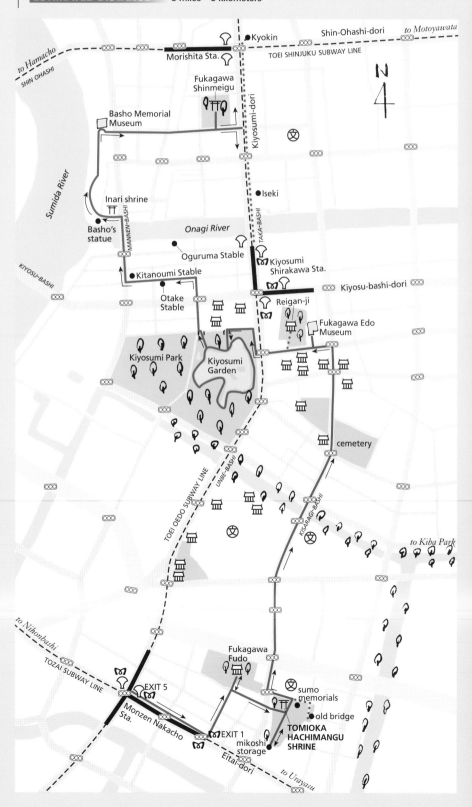

THE FUKAGAWA FESTIVAL

A full-scale festival is held every three years on the weekend closest to August 15, the next triennial years being 2008, 2011, and 2014. The festival-related events are simplified in intermediate years. The *mikoshi* parade on festival Sunday leaves the shrine at 7:30 and returns between 13:30 and 15:30. The neighborhoods of Monzen Naka-cho Station bustle with porters and spectators well before departure time. Those arriving late or opting to avoid the crowds should go to the intersection near Kiyosumi Shirakawa Station, where the parade will pass between 9:30 and 11:30. For more details, log onto www.tomiokahachimangu.or.jp.

journey to northern Japan—a travel experience that later crystallized in his renowned poetic diary, *The Narrow Road to the Deep North*.

Fukagawa was devastated twice in the space of twenty years in the 20th century—by the 1923 Kanto earthquake and World War II air raids. As fires devoured the area, few monuments escaped destruction. In the 1980s the lumber business moved farther south to Tokyo Bay's edge, leaving the empty sites to eager condominium and office building developers.

Fukagawa nevertheless has vestiges of its romantic history beneath its modern appearance. Refurbished riversides invite walkers for a leisurely stroll under broad skies—a real treat in overcrowded Tokyo. Local citizens, preserving what remains of the vibrant past, proudly point to the Fukagawa Edo Museum, a charming, small museum with an atmospheric presentation of the old Fukagawa lifestyle. The summer festival of Tomioka Hachimangu shrine offers a great opportunity to experience the animated, vigorous energy that continues to pulse throughout today's Fukagawa.

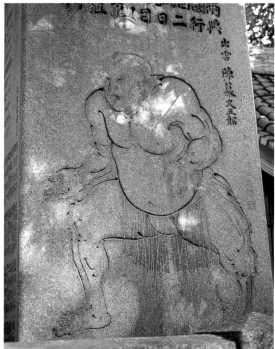

NOW

Our walk begins at Monzen Nakacho Station on the Tozai and Toei Oedo subway lines. The best place to start is Exit 1 of the Tozai Line station. If arriving by the Toei Oedo Line, use Exit 5, make a U-turn right on the street, and go left along Eitai-dori to find Exit 1 at the second traffic light.

TOP LEFT: Festive paper lantern hung under the eaves, Fukagawa.

TOP RIGHT: Stately main hall of Tomioka Hachimangu shrine.

BOTTOM: Mid-19th-century *yokozuna* sumo wrestler Jinmaku portrayed on a stone slab, Tomioka Hachimangu.

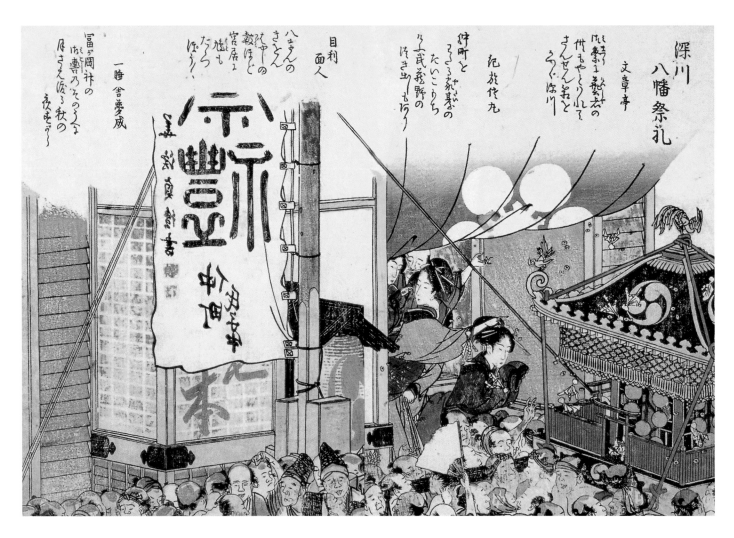

深川
八幡祭礼

文章亭

紀旅作丸

一睡舎夢成

目利
面人

Entering through a red gate by this subway exit, head toward Fukagawa Fudo temple, passing attractive souvenir shops and restaurants on both sides. Visit on one of the monthly fair days—the 1st, 15th, or 28th—and you will find yourself battling crowds of visitors and street hawkers.

The temple at the end of the approach radiates a sense of deep devotion, with worshippers immersed in prayer at the front and frequent, dramatic fire service incantations at the altar. You may enter the main hall if there is no ongoing major event, and take a self-guided tour following the arrow signs. The god Fudo, to whom the temple is dedicated, is a guardian of Buddhists under esoteric discipline. Believed to ward off evil spirits disturbing the ascetic training, this god is rendered as a god of justice, brandishing a sword in one hand and enveloped in flames of fury. Edo Kabuki actor Ichikawa Danjuro II (1688–1758) highly revered this god, and his depiction of Fudo on the stage became a huge success, which contributed significantly to Fudo's great popularity among Edo townspeople.

Leaving the temple, descend the steps and turn left to reach the west entrance to Tomioka Hachimangu shrine. The precinct, surrounded by thick foliage, is usually quiet but will be full of feverish excitement on its triennial summer festival day. Thousands of festival enthusiasts, donning traditional indigo coats and tight pants, scramble to carry *mikoshi* portable shrines. They march along the main streets, crossing over to the Sumida's west bank. Onlookers along the course throw buckets of water over them. Though symbolically intended to purify the porters, the splashes also serve as a much-welcomed relief from the strenuous exercise. The festival climaxes in the afternoon

when a procession of young costumed women joins in the parade, singing *kiyari*, a lumbermen's labor song.

A fabulous *mikoshi* is on display in a glass-walled building in a precinct corner closer to Eitai-dori. A gift in 1991 from Sagawa Kiyoshi (1922–2002), entrepreneurial chairman of Sagawa Kyubin express delivery company, the amazing structure, studded with diamonds and rubies, weighs a staggering 4.5 tons. The rooftop phoenix has 4-carat diamond eyes and a crest covered with 2,010 rubies, and the pair of wooden lions in the front have 3-carat diamond eyes.

In the rear garden, you will find massive stone monuments associated with sumo. A pair of slabs with linear carvings of wrestlers commemorate a famous 1857 match between Jinmaku (right) and Shiranui (left). Huge monoliths behind them are inscribed with all the names of *yokozuna*, the top-ranked wrestlers, from Akashi Shiganosuke, the legendary first *yokozuna* licensed in 1624, to the current ones. This shrine hosted more than thirty tournaments before Eko-in temple became the only venue to host sumo (see Ryogoku).

Leaving via the shrine's rear gate nearby, turn left, then right and go straight. Cross Kisaragi-bashi bridge, and walk to the third traffic light. Fukagawa Edo Museum to the left of the intersection offers the visitor the thrilling experience of stepping back in time into the Fukagawa of the 1830s. In the main gallery, visitors can stroll through a re-creation of a small riverside town, complete with shops, taverns, and people's homes, authentically reproduced in minute detail, including unseen parts of the buildings. The museum's appeal lies in its interactive style and realism—you can enter the houses and touch anything on display. Try on a raincoat made of rice straw or pretend to sip tea as you sit

TOP LEFT: Woodblock print (*ukiyo-e*) depicting the festival of Tomioka Hanchimangu. Print by Katsushika Hokusai (1760–1849)

BOTTOM LEFT: Nanawatari Benten shrine dedicated to a water goddess, Tomioka Hachimangu

TOP RIGHT: Japanese taverns circa 1830–40 reproduced at the Fukagawa Edo Museum.

on a bench. You can also read stories about the town in an English brochure available for ¥500. (Open 9:30–16:30; closed the second and fourth Mondays of each month, a week each in February and June, and government holidays at the year-end to January 1. Tel: 3630–8625.)

Leaving the museum, go right to cross Kiyosumi-dori and take the right-hand street to the entrance of Kiyosumi Garden. The beautiful traditional garden, including Kiyosumi Park in the next block, was initially one estate owned by lumber tycoon Kinokuniya Bunzaemon and by daimyo high lords. In the wake of the 1868 Meiji Restoration, Iwasaki Yataro (1834–85), founder of the Mitsubishi *zaibatsu* financial and industrial conglomerate, purchased it and created a luxurious guest house with a garden featuring numerous rocks of great rarity and variety. After the garden's verdant woods and water saved many people's lives during the 1923 earthquake, the Iwasaki family donated the whole property to the city. (Open 9:00–16:30; closed Mondays. The traditional guest house near the pond can be rented for private functions. Tel: 3641–5892.)

Exiting the garden via the front gate on the corner and bearing right, walk across Kiyosu-bashi-dori and take the first left. At the major street turn right to the Mannen-bashi bridge, spanning the Onagi-gawa river. The bridge in its old wooden structure was depicted in many *ukiyo-e* masterpieces by Hiroshige and Hokusai, who also included the majestic views of Mt. Fuji in the far west.

Off to the left of the bridge's other end, a small shrine with a red gate and red banners is dedicated to the Inari god and also commemorates the site of Basho's cottage in this area. At the end of the lane, a small park has been created on the very edge of the Sumida, tucked away behind another little shrine to propitiate the god of boils (*odeki*)! Ascending to an airy open terrace, visitors will be immediately drawn to Kiyosu-bashi bridge straddling the water's broad expanse. The hero in the scene, however, is a cast-bronze Basho gazing from his high pedestal at boats plying the river. The evocative arrangement commemorates the great traveler-poet perfectly, with bamboo bushes and banana trees rustling in the breeze.

Returning to the lane, bear left toward the river and pause at the top of the stairway to look for a green-roofed building ahead on the right. This is the Basho Memorial Museum, exhibiting archival materials and artifacts related to the poet. Stroll along the lower walkway and ascend via the next staircase to enter the museum from its rear gate. (Open 9:30–17:00; closed Mondays and during the New Year holiday.)

A small garden is landscaped to conjure the poet's famous ramblings through mountain trails. Basho aficionados will enjoy the museum exhibits, but be warned—no English explanations are provided. Exiting from the front gate, go straight to pass by Fukagawa Shinmeigu on the left. The tutelary shrine of northern Fukagawa villagers stands on the site of Fukagawa Hachiroemon's residence. The shrine celebrates its summer festival every three years, the next being 2009.

Turning left as you leave the shrine, return to Kiyosumi-dori, the first major street. You may choose to go right to reach Kiyosumi Shirakawa Station, or left to use Morishita Station on the Toei Shinjuku and Oedo Lines. A tile-roofed, single-story building just before the Onagi-gawa is Iseki, a restaurant specializing in *dojo*, small fresh-water fish and a favorite of Edo commoners. Its fillet, cooked with vegetables and egg, and served with rice and soup on the side, is a local delicacy. (Open 11:30–14:00, 16:30–20:20; closed Mondays. Ask for *nuki-nabe*.) Near Morishita Station, Kyokin *soba* restaurant offers excellent noodles and provincial sake (*jizake*). (Open 11:30–20:00; closed Mondays and the third Tuesdays and Wednesdays of the month.)

ABOVE: Kiyosumi Garden's traditionally landscaped grounds around a large, peaceful pond.

FAR LEFT: Stone marking the site of Basho's cottage.

CENTER: Bronze statue of Basho on the Sumida riverside.

RIGHT: Mannen-bashi bridge at the junction of the Onagi and Sumida rivers.

Tsukiji & Higashi Ginza

Fish, Kabuki, and More Fish

築地　東銀座

THEN

A tour of Tsukiji will give you an opportunity to feel the vibrant spirit of the Edokko (literally, "sons of Edo"), the proud citizens of the shogun's city. Life in densely populated Edo was not easy. Wits and agility were necessary to thrive in the highly competitive environment. Still, Edo's economic dynamism kept spirits high. With confidence in their creative ideas and honed skills, the Edokko rivaled the warrior elites as patrons of a new urban culture.

Home to the Tokyo Central Wholesale Market and the Kabukiza theater, Tsukiji provides a perfect stage for two of the most celebrated traditions of Edo—the fish market and Kabuki—to continue to thrive.

The area name, Tsukiji, means "constructed land," as it was reclaimed from the shallows of Edo Bay in the wake of the 1657 fire

that destroyed much of the city. The developed new land was originally allocated to daimyo lords for storage facilities and to Hongan-ji temple, whose original building had been lost to the fire. The daimyo created beautiful gardens on their spacious coastal properties, while the large roof of Tsukiji Hongan-ji, visible from offshore, served as the landmark for fishermen in the bay.

Sushi, an international phenomenon today, has its origins in the hearty appetite of 19th-century Edokko, who thrived on their fast-paced environment. Made in a matter of seconds from a small handful of vinegared rice and a slice of raw fish, it was a 19th-century precursor to fast food, peddled on the street for a quick energy pick-up. Gradually sushi became more elaborate. Originally, the method of making sushi was an ancient way to preserve fish using months-long fermented rice, but the rice was not eaten. Someone introduced vinegar to eliminate the fermentation process, and a man in Honjo on the Sumida River's east bank conceived the idea of assembling fresh fish and freshly cooked vinegared rice.

Kabuki reached its artistic zenith in Edo, where a bravado style

LEFT: Woodblock print depicting the bustling fish market at Nihonbashi. Detail of print by Utagawa Kuniyasu (1793–1854). RIGHT: Fishmonger and early-morning customers at Tsukiji.

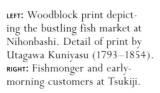

39

TSUKIJI & HIGASHI GINZA 築地－東銀座

NEAREST STATION   Tsukiji-shijo 築地市場 on the Toei Oedo Subway Line 都営大江戸線
or take a taxi to the Cosmo Gas Station on Shin-Ohashi-dori 新大橋通

ROUTE   The Jonai inner market 場内 (tuna auction site) ➡ restaurant area
魚河岸横丁 (Sushi Dai 寿司大, Daiwa-zushi 大和寿司, Aiyo coffee shop 愛養, Sushi Bun 鮨文,
Ryu-zushi 龍寿司, Iwasa-zushi 岩佐寿司) ➡ middlemen's section ➡ Namiyoke-jinja shrine
波除神社 ➡ Jogai outer market 場外 ➡ Hama Rikyu Gardens 浜離宮 or Tsukiji Hongan-ji temple
築地本願寺 ➡ Kabukiza theater 歌舞伎座 (Tatsuden kimono and bags 龍伝, Kabukiya doll shop
かぶき屋) ➡ Higashi Ginza Station 東銀座駅

ESTIMATED TIME   35 minutes (main route only)

ESTIMATED DISTANCE   1 ½ miles • 2 ½ kilometers (main route only)

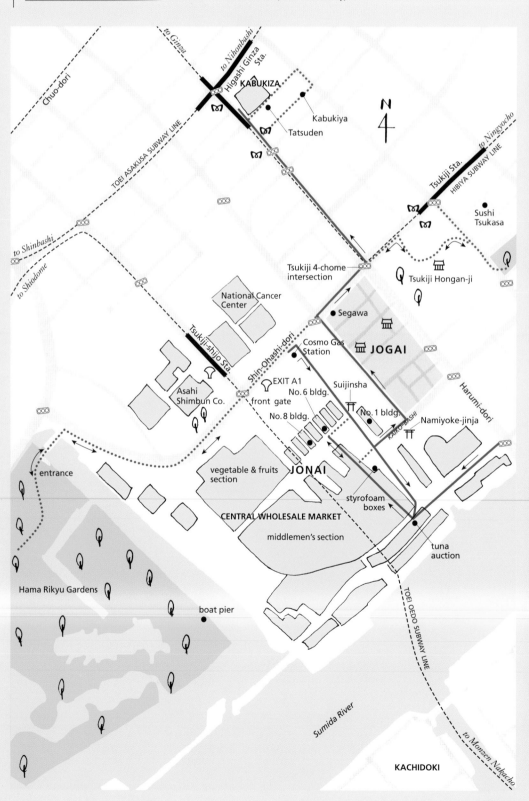

of drama called *aragoto* was developed with emphasis on power and speed. The classical theater of Japan originated in sensual street dances around the year 1600. Incorporating elements of Bunraku puppetry, Noh ritual dramas, and diverse folk performances, Kabuki gradually grew into a complex, independent theatrical genre. In the Kyoto and Osaka areas, audiences favored graceful presentations of romantic young men, and this style was named *wagoto*. Edokko preferred acts of rough bravery to match the brisk atmosphere of their newly built city. They enthusiastically applauded the Kabuki stars Ichikawa Danjuro and Danjuro II for their enactment of young heroes motivated by righteous indignation in the *aragoto* style.

NOW

An early-morning tour of Tsukiji is a must-do in Tokyo, starting with the tuna auctions. Head for the inner market, called Jonai. It is an arena of professionals vying with speed and efficiency to buy and sell fish. Be quick on your feet and watch out for a maelstrom of motor vehicles speeding in all directions. Beware of wet, greasy floors, too. The market is closed on Sundays, national holidays, and two-to-three arbitrarily chosen Wednesdays a month. Check the market calendar by logging on to www.tsukiji-market.or.jp.

The sights inside the tuna auction area are amazing. Rows of white-frosted tuna lie motionless on the concrete floor, shrouded by a cold mist. With heads and tails chopped off, they resemble logged timbers or even granite torsos. Some men move them around to change the orders, others bend over to check the ruby-red meat exposed from the cut-off tail ends. Labels indicate the respective place of origin, such as LO for Los Angeles and SD for Sydney. Numbers written in red are codes for auctioning. As you watch, you might sense a quiet tension gradually building in the air. Suddenly, a hand bell signals that the first wholesaler is ready to start. The auctioneer and bidders frantically exchange mumbled words and hand signs. Ten minutes later, all the deals have been cut, and the hapless spectators generally have no clue what has occurred.

After the tuna auctions, there will be a lull before the middlemen occupying some nine hundred booths are ready for shoppers. Thus, a break at the restaurant area might be a good idea. More than a hundred shops and restaurants are packed together along narrow lanes in the Jonai market. Cut straight across the middlemen's area and look for red numbers above eye level on the walls of narrow buildings. The No. 6 building has two sushi restaurants—Sushi Dai and Daiwa-zushi. Next to Sushi Dai, Aiyo is popular for good coffee and buttered toast with jam or marmalade. The No. 8 building has Sushi Bun, famous for its delicately cooked *anago* (conger) and *shinko* (baby gizzards shad; in season in June and July). The No. 1 building to the right as you face Suijinsha shrine also has two sushi restaurants, Ryu-zushi, the sixth unit from the left, and Iwasa-zushi, marked by an orange curtain.

Tuna auction at the Tsukiji wholesale market.

HOW TO GET THERE

Arriving by taxi on Harumi-dori, you should get off just before Kachidoki-bashi, the last bridge on the Sumida River. Turn right and walk straight to a beige-colored building, looking for a door on its right-hand side with a sign saying VISITOR PASSAGE ENTRANCE.

If you arrive on Shin-Ohashi-dori, get off in front of the Cosmo Gas Station and take the left-hand street to reach the same building beyond a pile of styrofoam boxes. Notice a small shrine, Suijinsha, along the way on the left, which is dedicated to the god of water. Try to be there around 5:15 A.M., as the tuna auctions start at 5:30 A.M. Alternatively, you may use the Toei Oedo Line, though you will arrive barely in time for the auctions. The first morning train arrives at Tsukiji-shijo Station around 5:20. Take Exit A1 and turn right to find Cosmo Gas Station ahead, where you should turn right and follow the aforementioned directions.

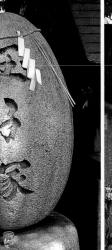

TOP LEFT: Carved wood lion head, replica of an Edo-period original, Namiyoke-jinja.

TOP RIGHT: Paper lantern, Namiyoke-jinja.

CENTER: Stones in the Namiyoke-jinja garden offered in thanks for commodities sold in the market, including eggs (*left*), sushi (*middle*), and shrimp (*right*).

BOTTOM: Shoppers stroll through the stalls of the Jogai outer market.

FACING PAGE, TOP: A beautiful plate of sushi, prepared fresh from the market at Sushi Tsukasa (see map), one of the many Tsukiji sushi restaurants.

FACING PAGE, BOTTOM: Sake kegs offered to the gods of Namiyoke-jinja.

Business in the middlemen's area peaks around 8:00 when chefs come to buy, usually, from their favorite middlemen. Though housed under a huge roof, the booths have changed little from the makeshift structures at the Nihonbashi fish market depicted in Edo-period (1600–1868) prints. Fish are spread out on wooden boards or in boxes in front, and payments are settled at a small desk in the back. Shoppers and workers hustle around elbow to elbow as they pass by on narrow lanes. The customers and traders, seemingly chatting or joking, are actually negotiating earnestly with sharp eyes for the best quality and best price, so please be alert and do not disturb them! The quantity and diversity of fish are overwhelming. The market attracts about 450 kinds of fish from all over Japan and the world, averaging 2,300 tons and ¥1.8 billion (US$15.5 million) in daily sales.

Adjacent to the Jonai market, the Jogai (outer market) is open until about 13:00, giving amateur chefs more time to look around. The two markets are linked by a bridge named Kaiko-bashi, which formerly spanned a canal emptying into the Sumida River.

The shrine by the bridge is Namiyoke-jinja, housed in the main hall built in 1659. Workers often stop here to pray. Huge wooden lion heads enshrined inside the *torii* gate on both sides are reproductions of a pair of male (right) and female (left) wooden sculptures believed since the Edo period to have divine power to expel evil spirits. Contemporary worshippers at the shrine also include engineers in bridge and ship construction as well as those in the ongoing reclamation of Tokyo Bay.

Along the street leading directly away from the shrine, the Jogai market consists of about four hundred shops occupying several blocks. Increasingly tough competition with supermarket chains, franchised restaurants, and online companies has forced some of them to close down or change hands, but many have retained their highly specialized businesses. The small eateries along Shin-Ohashi-dori are prospering from a quick turnover of customers. One of them, Segawa, serves just *maguro donburi*, soy-flavored tuna sashimi on vinegared

TOP: Ichikawa Danjuro XII in *Shibaraku* (Just a Moment), a Kabuki play first staged by Danjuro I in 1697.

RIGHT: Kabukiza theater, a fine example of Japanese baroque architecture.

FAR RIGHT: Ichikawa Danjiro XII (*left*) as the hero Sukeroku, the champion of Edo commoners, in the play *Sukeroku Yukari no Edo-zakura*, with his lover Agemaki (*right*, played by Nakamura Jakuemon), a celebrated courtesan of the Yoshiwara red-light pleasure quarters.

rice in a bowl, a good choice for those who find a full set of sushi too heavy for breakfast.

From the Tsukiji 4-chome intersection, the Kabukiza theater is an easy 5-minute walk, three large blocks away. Since the theater opens at 10:30, you will have a couple of extra hours to kill. You have two interesting options. You can either visit the Hama Rikyu Teien (Hama Rikyu Gardens), which opens at 9:00, or explore the neighborhoods of Tsukiji Hongan-ji.

To reach the Hama Rikyu Garden, backtrack to the Cosmo Gas station and keep walking straight for about 10 minutes. As you approach the garden entrance to the left of the traffic light, you will notice the stone-buttressed walls similar to those of the Imperial Palace, or Edo Castle. Created as the beachside (*hama*) villa (*rikyu*) for the Tokugawa shoguns, the garden has a large tidal pond with a lovely pavilion in its center. Though the surrounding highrises inevitably intrude on the view, the verdant, spacious garden still affords the delights of wandering about and enjoying seasonal flowers. From the pier in the garden's northeastern corner, boats leave for a 35-minute cruise on the Sumida River to Asakusa (see Asakusa tour).

The front gate of Tsukiji Hongan-ji lies on Shin-Ohashi-dori. The main hall is open to the public when not being used for rituals. Exiting from its left-hand side gate and turning right, you will find a peaceful park for strolling.

The Kabukiza's ornate façade is unmistakable. Tickets for one act from the upper gallery are available at the left-hand booth with a sign overhead, BOX OFFICE FOR ONE SHOW. Visit the theater's web site at www.kabuki-za.co.jp., for information on the month's programs.

If you have a little time before the house opening, you might enjoy looking around the neighborhood. On the right-hand street as you face the theater, the Tatsuden shop teems with brocade bags and kimono materials, with bamboo poles flanking its narrow entrance to the basement store. Down the second street nearer the market almost to its end is the Kabukiya store, exhibiting lovely traditional dolls.

NOTE

■ The fish market will move in 2012 to Toyosu, 1¼ miles (2 kilometers) to the southeast.

■ The Kabukiza theater will be closed for reconstruction beginning in the near future. The new building will feature a three-gabled façade after the theater's 1924 original structure, combined with a 450-foot (140-meter) office building at its rear.

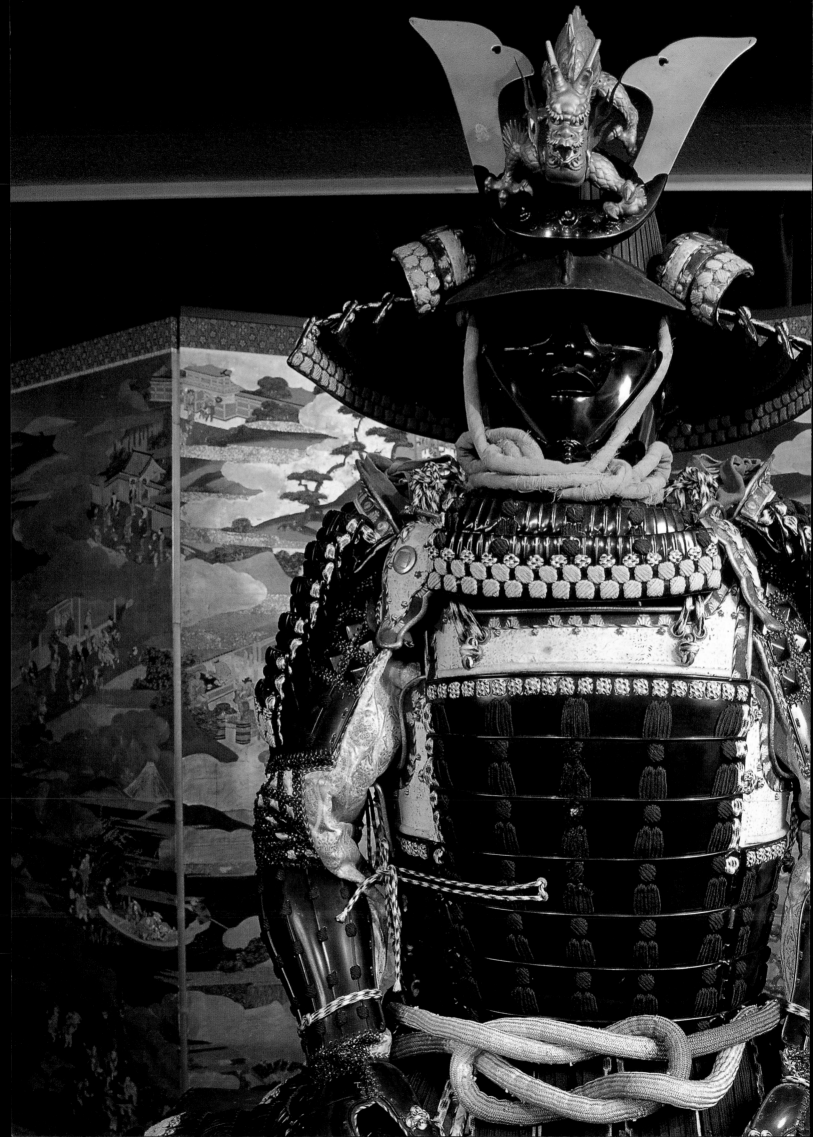

Atagoyama & Shiba

Samurai Feats and Traces of Shoguns Past

愛宕山 芝

THEN

In *The Capital of the Tycoon*, published in 1863, author Rutherford Alcock (1809–97), the first British government representative to Japan, gives a lively account of his experiences in Japan from 1859 to 1862. In a vivid description of a horse ride he took with his colleagues to explore the city of Edo, he mentions an amazing stairway and the great view from the top:

> Through the gateway may be seen the double flights of steps, the one leading up to the top of the hill, in a perpendicular and unbroken line; the other curving less abruptly upward. And, although the height is probably the same, the undulating flight looks so much less arduous, that we instinctively turn to the right, willing to believe in its gentler promise.
>
> And thus we gain the summit of Atagoyama, so called from the god Atago, to whom a temple is dedicated here. From no other point can so fine and commanding a view of the Bay of Edo, and the city washed by its waves, be obtained. And the picture that bursts suddenly upon the traveler is very striking. The hill fronts to the bay, but with a couple of miles of valley intervening, thickly covered by streets and temples. To the left, and in a northwestern direction, another two miles interval of plain is in like manner filled up with a dense mass of houses, until a range of hills is reached on which the Tycoon's castle stands.

Only 1 mile (1.6 kilometers) south of the Imperial Palace, the hill of Atagoyama is a narrow strip of land projecting from the Azabu Upland toward Tokyo Bay and over coastal areas reclaimed from the sea. The "streets and temples" and "dense mass of houses" Alcock saw were the residences of both daimyo and commoners in present-day Shinbashi, Hibiya, and Otemachi. Though the view from the hilltop Alcock found so memorable has since been lost to surrounding highrise buildings, the 86-step, 40-degree flight that confronted him remains, along with many anecdotes of samurai horse riders who masterfully challenged the formidable ascent and often successfully descended it as well.

The most famous story, passed down through generations of storytellers, has it that in 1634, Magaki Heikuro swiftly rode his horse up and down the grade to fetch branches of plum blossoms from the hilltop for the third shogun, Tokugawa Iemitsu. Iemitsu was returning to his castle from Zojo-ji temple, where his father, the second shogun, Hidetada, was buried. Looking up the steep stairway, Iemitsu asked

An elaborate suit of samurai armor, the Japan Sword Company.

his retinue if anyone would get the flowers for him, and Magaki immediately obliged and sped up the stairs on his horse.

While Magaki is considered to be a fictitious character, and some historians even doubt the existence of the stone stairway at that time, Atagoyama was nevertheless the apparent prime stage in Edo to show off equestrian artistry.

In 1925, Iwaki Toshio, a veteran Imperial Army stableman, rode his mount to the top of the stairs in less than a minute—though it took forty-five minutes to make the precipitous descent as the anxious audience looked on, holding their breath. Successfully returning, the brave horse almost collapsed and only recovered after a lengthy rest.

The dangers of these fabled feats still thrill and inspire visitors today as they look down from the top of the stairway.

Some distance south of Atagoyama, Zojo-ji was appointed by Tokugawa Ieyasu in 1590 to be his family's burial temple. This crowning glory was divided later with Kan'ei-ji temple, built in Ueno in 1625, the two temples thereafter vying for subsequent shoguns' mortuary rights. Zojo-ji's palatial premises and architectural splendor once spread over the southern edge of the Azabu Upland facing Edo Bay. Wartime bombings destroyed all but three gates. Much of the vacant site was sold or otherwise ceded to modern hotels, Tokyo Tower, and Shiba Koen park, while the temple has reserved a central portion of the land for itself.

TOP LEFT: Toranomon Sunaba *soba* restaurant operates from a one-hundred-year-old wooden home.

TOP RIGHT: Fresh *soba* noodles, Toranomon Sunaba.

RIGHT: Exquisitely crafted *biwa* lutes, Ishida Biwaten.

FAR RIGHT: Lute maker Ishida-san at work.

ATAGOYAMA & SHIBA 愛宕山−芝

NEAREST STATION   Toranomon 虎ノ門 on the Ginza Subway Line 銀座線

ROUTE   Toranomon Sunaba *soba* noodle restaurant 虎ノ門砂場 ➡ Ishida Biwaten Japanese lute shop 石田琵琶店 ➡ Japan Sword Company 日本刀剣 ➡ Atago-jinja shrine 愛宕神社 ➡ Restaurant T. ➡ Shiba Koen Park 芝公園 ➡ Tofuya Ukai tofu restaurant とうふ屋うかい ➡ Zojo-ji temple 増上寺 ➡ Daimon Station 大門駅 or JR Hamamatsucho Station 浜松町駅

OPTION   Shiba Toshogu shrine 芝東照宮 ➡ Shiba Koen Station 芝公園駅

ESTIMATED TIME   65 minutes

ESTIMATED DISTANCE   2¾ miles • 4½ kilometers

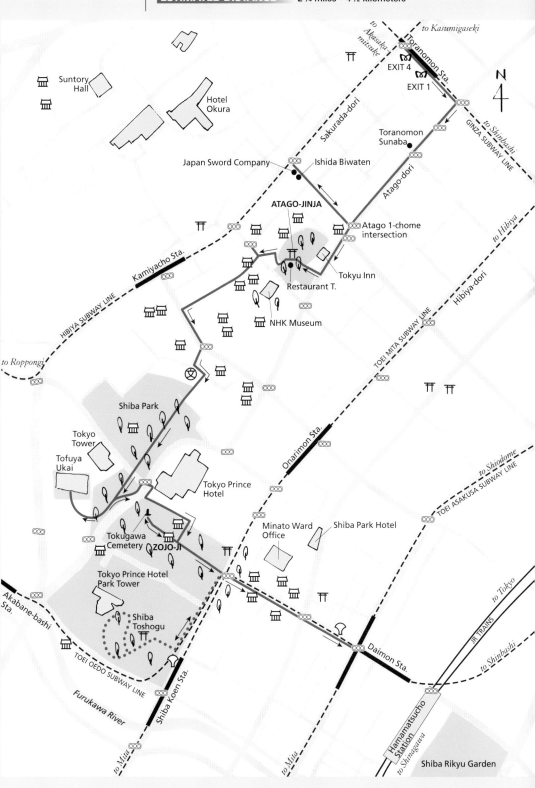

NOW

We begin our walk at Toranomon Station on the Ginza Subway Line. From Exit 1 or 4, walk straight to the traffic light and turn right. Two small blocks ahead is a *soba* noodle restaurant, Toranomon Sunaba. It is located in a vintage wooden house and boasts around a hundred years in business at this site. (Open 11:00–21:30 on weekdays, 11:00–15:00 on Saturdays; closed Sundays and holidays.) Simple, finely sliced buckwheat noodles (*soba*) were a great favorite of the Edo commoners. Reportedly, about half of the 6,100 restaurants in Edo in the 1830s specialized in *soba*.

Proceeding on the main street, turn right at the next traffic light of Atago 1-chome intersection to take a short detour to two unique shops—Ishida Biwaten and the Japan Sword Company. The former is the only store in Japan to offer custom-made *biwa*—Japanese lutes plucked with a plectrum—helping to sustain the growing attention the instrument is receiving in modern music. (Open 9:00–17:00; closed Sundays and holidays.) Introduced from China in the 8th century, the fretted, stringed instrument had a distinct evolution. The *biwa* was associated with religious chants in Buddhist rituals and with wandering entertainers' recitations of military romances. The golden age of *biwa* came in the 16th century. After a period of decline, the *biwa* owes its revival in the 20th century to Takemitsu Toru (1930–96), who wrote many ensembles for *biwa*, *shakuhachi* flute, and orchestra, including the internationally famous *November Steps* written for the New York Philharmonic Orchestra to celebrate its 125th anniversary in 1967.

The Japan Sword Company on Sakurada-dori has galleries on the second and third floors, available for viewing upon request. Antique swords, war helmets, armor, and decorative silk screens conjure up a world of martial valor, honor, and stoic discipline. (Open 9:30–18:00; closed on Sundays and holidays.)

Backtracking to the Atago 1-chome intersection, turn right to find the brown *torii* gate of Atago-jinja set back from the street. The grueling, steep ascent to the hilltop at eighty-five feet (twenty-six meters) above sea level will be rewarded by the delightful sight of an idyllic, peaceful pond set in a grove of old evergreens and flowering cherry trees. A small wooden boat is moored near rocks, and an array of carp swim about in the rippling waters.

A famous, aged plum tree, now almost completely withered, lives on, a reminder of the earlier times of Magaki's legendary ride. It stands behind a fenced-in garden to the left of the red gate bearing the Tokugawa crest of three mallow leaves.

The little shrine boasts an affiliation with the first Tokugawa shogun, Ieyasu. Originally a Buddhist temple founded in 1603 for devotion to his long-cherished statue of the god Jizo, it became associated later with the god of Atago-jinja in northwestern Kyoto, whose power offered protection from fire—a blessing vital to Edo, a city of wood and paper houses.

A wonderful recent addition to the shrine premises is Restaurant T., a one-story building of light-colored wood near the hand-washing stand. T. serves simple but mouthwatering lunches on a first-come, first-served basis. The restaurant's name stands for Tokyo and, true to its namesake, though never explicitly declared by the owner, everything here, from the drinks and the ingredients in the food to the tableware, is purportedly from Tokyo. Reservations may be made for the evening. (Open 11:30–14:00, 17:00–21:30; closed Mondays; Tel: 5777–5557; weekends often reserved for parties.)

The four-story white building nearby, the NHK Museum, commemorates the first radio broadcasting station opened in Japan in 1925. Walking toward it, look for a steel ladder on the right, diagonally

LEFT: Full shot and detail of an exotic drum for *gagaku* court dance, Atago-jinja.

ABOVE: Interior of the restaurant Tofuya Ukai (also seen on the front jacket) and a sample from their menu.

across the paths as you exit the shrine. Make a zigzag descent through the undeveloped woody hillside. Reaching the street, cross it and continue walking to the T-junction ahead, where you should turn left. At the next traffic light, cross the street and go uphill, turning left at the hilltop and soon taking a lane to the right that leads into Shiba Koen park.

Cut across the park and its continuation in the next block below Tokyo Tower. Emerging out of the dense, shady woods, you will find an atmospheric restaurant, Tofuya Ukai, the rustic elegance of its earthen-walled gate lending a stunning contrast with the 1,100-foot (333-meter), steel-framed landmark tower as a backdrop. As you enter, cordially ushered in by an attendant dressed in kimono, you will have the overwhelming sense that you have stepped back in time to a bygone age—with the mellow, lacquered interior of the entrance hall, a slowly rotating water mill in the verdant garden, and white paper lanterns beginning to glow in the evening dusk. The menu offers elaborate *kaiseki*-style courses specializing in tofu. The restaurant is pricy but well worth a visit. (Open 11:00–20:00 throughout the year. Lunch is served until 15:00. Tel: 3436–1028; www.ukai. co.jp/shiba/index.html.)

Leaving the restaurant, backtrack to the park's northeastern corner with a traffic light on the right and cross the intersection to the Tokyo Prince Hotel side. Bear right to take a wooded lane separating the hotel from Zojo-ji.

Entering Zojo-ji on your right, you will be drawn to hundreds of small identical statues, each with a pinwheel rattling in the wind. These stones are offerings given by bereaved parents to pray for happiness in the other world for their infants who have met untimely deaths. Glancing at the majestic main hall, rebuilt in 1974, bear right to go around the wooden hall closer to the hedges, finding the current Tokugawa cemetery behind a tightly closed gate. Here now lie six of the fifteen Tokugawa shoguns of Japan, including their spouses and relatives, who were moved and reburied after the grand old mausoleums on both sides of Zojo-ji were lost to wartime bombings. The gate doors with the Tokugawa crest are flanked by brass panels embossed with great dragon designs. Nearby stand several stone statues in a row with enigmatic smiles as if to soften the austere silence of the cemetery.

Back at the main hall, head toward the massive San-mon front gate to exit, admiring the grandeur still emanating the energy of the original 1620s construction. A Himalayan cedar on the left provides a balance with the wooden edifice, having grown to an enormous size since its planting by Ulysses Simpson Grant, 18th President of the United States, in memory of his visit to Japan in 1879.

Exiting the gate, you can reach Daimon Station on the Toei Oedo and Asakusa Lines, or JR Hamamatsucho Station, both straight ahead.

Turning right from the San-mon, however, you will find a path just before the entrance to the Shiba Koen Subway Station leading to Shiba Toshogu, one of a series of shrines dedicated to the deified first Tokugawa shogun, Ieyasu. The shrine is a much-diminished postwar reconstruction, but the ginkgo on its right is a survivor of the inferno of six decades ago. The 81-foot (25-meter) arboreal giant is splendid when clad in golden yellow in late November to early December.

TOP LEFT: Zojo-ji temple and Tokyo Tower as dusk falls.

BOTTOM LEFT: Memorial stone in honor of Edo fire brigade Me-gumi, Zojo-ji.

CENTER: Temple bell, Zojo-ji.

TOP RIGHT: Old ginkgo sparkling in sunlight filtering through its golden leaves, Shiba Toshogu shrine.

BOTTOM RIGHT: Shiba Toshogu shrine, restored after World War II.

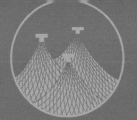

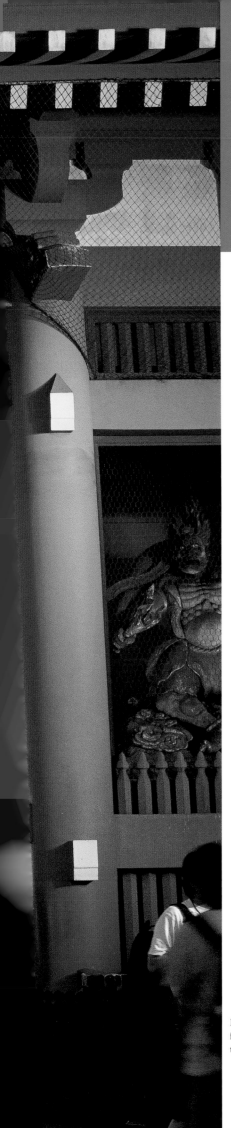

Asakusa

A Classic Temple District, with Shops and Festivities

浅草

THEN

Asakusa Kannon, the most famous Buddhist temple in Tokyo, has been a people's temple since antiquity—for almost 1,400 years.

Legend has it that the temple's god manifested itself as a small statue netted by two poor fishermen brothers on the Sumida River. Thinking it no more than a piece of junk, they threw it back, even though it was their only "catch" of the day. Upon returning home, they were dismayed to learn from the village elder that what they had passed off as mere junk was in fact the image of the venerable Kannon, the Buddhist god of mercy. Buddhism advocates the sanctity of all life, and fishing is a forbidden act of killing. Fearing vengeance from the god, the brothers and the elder hurried to dedicate an altar to the statue and prayed earnestly for pardon of the brothers' sin, an ignorant rather than malicious act. The next day, the brothers, having no other means of supporting themselves, reluctantly returned to the river to fish and, to their amazement, were blessed with the best catch of their lives!

This extraordinary tale, dating from 628 A.D., propagates an enduring belief that the Kannon of Asakusa came to save the ignorant poor from their sins and sufferings. The power of widespread faith has enabled Asakusa Kannon, or Senso-ji (the temple's formal name), to attain eminence in the region since the 10th century. Prominent military leaders, such as Minamoto no Yoritomo (1147–99), showed their reverence for this temple with generous donations, a tradition continued by Tokugawa Ieyasu (1543–1616) and subsequent Tokugawa shoguns. Notwithstanding the patronage of the elite, Senso-ji has always embraced ordinary people, allowing shops and entertainers to enliven its premises. The result is a perennial festival-like bustle that almost overshadows the temple edifices, quite unlike the stoic serenity of typical temple grounds.

In 1657 the infamous Yoshiwara red-light pleasure quarters moved from central Edo (see Nihonbashi) to a patch of rice fields a short distance away from the temple, bringing nightlife to Asakusa's prosperity. Kabuki theaters, also relocated in 1841, boosted the area's already significant reputation in performing arts. With the advent of the Western operetta and movies in the early 20th century, the temple's west side became Japan's foremost hub of modern entertainment. Though only the crumbling shells of the old theaters remain today, at one time this area drew crowds of mostly lower-class patrons, who were happy to spend their rare holidays in Asakusa with a little extra money in their pockets.

Kaminari-mon, the all-too-famous front gate of Asakusa Kannon temple, also known as Senso-ji.

NOW

Its former glory mostly faded, Asakusa is still a magnet for sight-seers in Tokyo, especially for those on a tight schedule. The colorful shopping lanes are fun just to wander about. The wide range of goods from trinkets to real gems allows travelers to find ideal gifts for friends and family.

First-time visitors should use the Ginza Line Asakusa Station—take Exit 1 or 3 and walk one block straight ahead to Kaminari-mon, Senso-ji's impressive front gate. Passing under the huge, much photographed paper lantern, enter Nakamise, the main shopping street leading to the majestic main hall. This lane alone houses around a hundred shops, with hundreds more spread throughout a large square surrounding the temple. Among the bewildering array of shops, several continue to deal in authentic, traditional products, such as Kaneso cutlery and Bunsendo fans, which can be found in the second lane to the left after passing through the gate. The most fascinating of

all the stores is Sukeroku, the second shop from the temple end of Nakamise on the right. Thousands of ingeniously crafted Edo-style toys and miniatures fill the display shelves of the six-foot-wide (two-meter) shop space.

Facing Sukeroku is a series of pictures on glass-covered signposts along the garden fence. These pictures narrate, from left to right, the myth of the temple's foundation. Following the fence around to the left and then to the right, you can explore the recently refurbished Denboin-dori, another shopping street. Notice Yonoya comb shop, almost three hundred years old, on the left. Traditional hair ornaments and combs in the window are fascinating just to look at. Handcrafted combs made with quality boxwood are expensive, but their wonderful smooth surfaces continue to lure connoisseurs.

Returning to the front of Sukeroku, note the large, impressive gate nearby. This is the Hozo-mon (Treasure Storage Gate), so called because its upper story is a repository for Holy Scriptures and other temple treasures. Beyond the gate is the main hall, and off to the left soars the red-and-gold pagoda. All these are post–World War II ferroconcrete reconstructions erected after their wooden originals were lost to the air raids of 1945.

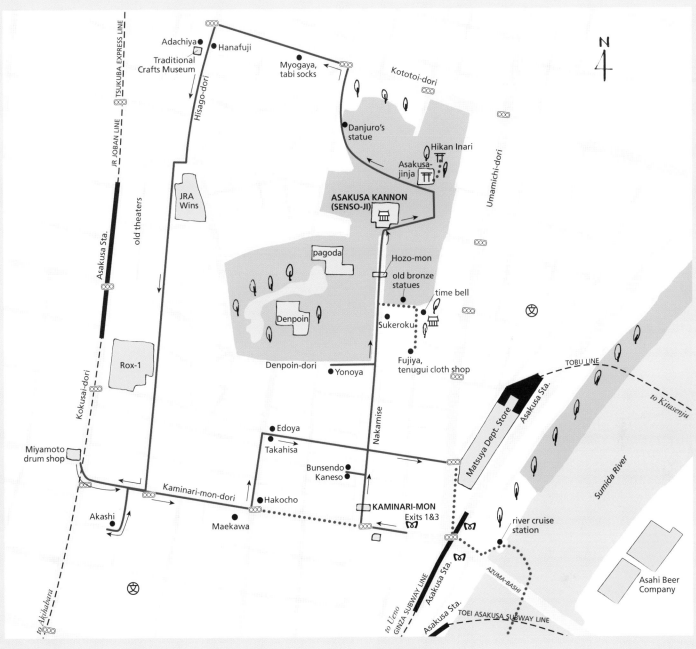

N

ASAKUSA 浅草

NEAREST STATION Asakusa 浅草 on the Ginza Subway Line 銀座線 or Toei Asakusa Subway Line 都営浅草線

ROUTE Kaminari-mon gate 雷門 ➡ Nakamise 仲見世 (Kaneso cutlery かね惣, Bunsendo fans 文扇堂; Sukeroku the toys and miniatures 助六) ➡ Yonoya combs よのや ➡ Hozo-mon gate 宝蔵門 ➡ Asakusa Kannon Main Hall 浅草観音 ➡ Asakusa-jinja 浅草神社 ➡ Danjuro's statue ➡ Hisago-dori (Adachiya festival outfits あだちや, Hanafuji paper lanterns 花藤, Traditional Crafts Museum 下町伝統工芸館) ➡ Miyamoto *mikoshi* & drum shop 宮本卯之助商店 ➡ Akashi tempura restaurant あかし ➡ Maekawa deer-hide bags 前川 ➡ Hakocho decorative wooden boxes 箱長 ➡ Takahisa souvenirs 高久 ➡ Edoya souvenirs 江戸屋 ➡ Matsuya Department Store 松屋 ➡ Asakusa Station (in basement of Matsuya) 浅草駅

OPTION Sumida River cruise to Hama Rikyu Gardens 浜離宮

ESTIMATED TIME 40 minutes

ESTIMATED DISTANCE 1 ½ miles • 2.5 kilometers

TOP: Classic Japanese fans, Bunsendo.

MIDDLE: *Nakamise* shopping street of Senso-ji.

BOTTOM: Shoppers in summer *yukata*.

Proceed to the main hall of Senso-ji, passing a large bronze incense burner. People gather here to waft the smoke emanating from the incense to various areas of their bodies, with the belief that the holy smoke will cure ailments.

The spacious main hall attracts a constant stream of worshippers. They throw coins in the offering box and pray with their hands together to the original fishermen's statue of Kannon supposedly enshrined in the glittering gold inner shrine. Though no evidence of the statue's actual existence has been found, proof matters little before the timeless power of belief. The temple itself has existed since the 7th century. Roof tiles and other artifacts from a post–World War II archaeological excavation substantiate the date.

Leaving the main hall, go left to visit the adjacent Asakusa-jinja dedicated to the three founding fathers of Senso-ji: the two brothers and their village elder. The famous Sanja-matsuri festival in May is the occasion for the shrine's parish members to pay tribute to their ancient patriarchs. Notice a crest of three fishing nets on the door of the right-hand warehouse storing the three *mikoshi* portable shrines, representing the three deified villagers.

The beautiful main building, one of the few architectural survivors of World War II, was donated by the third shogun, Tokugawa Iemitsu, in 1649. Built in the decorative *gongen-zukuri* style typical of a Shinto shrine dedicated to a posthumously deified person,

SHRINE BLESSING

For the blessing (*go-kito*), a priest will escort you to the waiting room and ask you to fill out a form indicating your name, address, and wishes. Choose one of the traditional themes such as family happiness (*kanai anzen*), business prosperity (*shobai hanjo*), or good health (*shintai kenko*) and make your other specific wishes when praying in front of the altar. Quietly follow the priest to the inner sanctuary and stand with your head down during most of the ritual. Toward the end of the service, you will be invited to move forward to present a sacred branch at the altar. The basic manner of worship in front of the altar is to bow twice, clap your hands twice, and bow once more. Holding the branch upright, say your prayers silently, turn the branch clockwise, and place it on the table with the bottom end toward the altar. Leaving the altar area, you will receive a sip of sacred saké from the priest. A donation of ¥3,000 or more is customary.

LEFT: Hozo-mon gate (*left*) and Goju-no-To pagoda (*right*), authentic reconstructions.

ABOVE: A rickshaw with a guide in traditional garb.

BOTTOM LEFT: *Nakamise* shops at twilight.

BOTTOM RIGHT: Visitors to Senso-ji fanning the "healing smoke" of the incense toward themselves.

Asakusa-jinja features complex roof lines and colorfully painted ornaments on the pillars and walls. The shrine offers visitors the opportunity to receive a ritual blessing by a priest in the lavishly decorated altar area. Anyone can apply at the right-hand booth or nearby door. (Press the buzzer if no one is around and follow the instructions on page 61.)

After visiting Asakusa-jinja, you may wish to wander freely because there is so much to discover. Time permitting, try to explore the temple's less-frequented north and west sides.

At the far corner of the main temple's rear ground stands a splendid statue of Ichikawa Danjuro IX, a Kabuki celebrity in the 1930s. Past Danjuro's statue, turn right to reach Kototoi-dori and go left, then left again at the next traffic light, and enter Hisago-dori, an arcaded street tinged with an ambience of prewar Tokyo. On the right, the Adachiya festival outfit shop enjoys continued patronage by festival buffs. Across the street from Adachiya, Hanafuji sells small paper lanterns. The two *kanji* characters for Asakusa are already written on them, and the shop owner can add any name to order—perfect souvenirs from your Asakusa adventure.

A few buildings ahead, Edo Shitamachi Dento Kogei-kan (Traditional Crafts Museum) exhibits traditional handicrafts by contemporary artisans from Taito-ku. This ward is home to about one hundred artisans with diverse skills, whose portraits decorate the lobby wall. Examples of their works are shown in the lobby and on the second floor. Among the displayed items are wooden furniture and chests made using traditional joinery. Beautifully crafted without nails, these Edo *sashimono* are treasured for their expression of the natural beauty of wood. Exhibited items are not for sale, but with the gallery attendant's help you can contact the artisan and place an order. Artisans demonstrate crafts every weekend. (Open 10:00–20:00

TOP: Offerings on a raised tray, near Denpo-in.

BOTTOM: Fox guardian at Hikan Inari shrine behind Asakusa-jinja.

RIGHT: Miniature foxes offered by worshippers, Hikan Inari shrine.

throughout the year. Tel: 3842–1990; www.city.taito.tokyo.jp.)

Bear right at the end of Hisago-dori and walk straight to Kaminari-mon-dori, where you should go right and cross Kokusai-dori to visit Miyamoto Unosuke Shoten (Japanese Percussion & Festival Store), renowned supplier of everything you need to organize a Japanese festival. Walk in for a close look at the *mikoshi* portable shrines and *taiko* drums carefully handcrafted at their workshop nearby. Taiko-kan on the fourth floor is a hands-on drum museum—a great favorite of children. Be careful not to touch the delicate ones marked with a red circle. (Open 10:00–17:00; closed Mondays and Tuesdays. Tickets to the drum museum are available at the desk on the first floor.)

After exploring Miyamoto, walk straight back to the subway station on Kaminari-mon-dori. If you have worked up an appetite with all that walking, you can stop for a tempura lunch at nearby Akashi, a family-operated restaurant accessible by taking the first right on Kaminari-mon-dori and turning right again. Ask for *jo-teishoku*, piping hot tempura with rice and miso soup on the side. (Open 11:30–14:30; 17:00–21:00; closed Sundays and holidays. Tel: 3841–0788.)

Close to the second traffic light, Maekawa specializes in handbags, pouches, and business-card holders made of deer hide. Called *inden*, the smooth, suedelike skin dyed and stencil-patterned with natural *urushi* lacquer was first used to decorate

LEFT: *Hagoita*, traditional battledores decorated with padded figures of Kabuki characters.

BELOW: A lovely pouch made of deer skin decorated in the *inden* technique, Maekawa.

armor, war helmets, and sword sheaths. In peaceful Edo, gentlemen treasured tobacco and money pouches made of the lightweight yet durable material. (Open 10:00–18:00; closed Wednesdays.)

For the last detour, cross Kaminari-mon-dori at the traffic light and go straight, soon finding Hakocho on the right, offering wooden boxes and drawers with attractive designs of inlaid silk cloth.

At the third lane ahead, turn right to explore two shops teeming with Edo-style souvenirs—Takahisa on the right and Edoya on the left. Continuing straight, you will cross Nakamise and reach Matsuya Department Store, where you can find the Ginza Line's Asakusa Station entrance in the basement.

Time and weather permitting, you can cruise back to central Tokyo on the Sumida, enjoying the river breeze. The cruise ends at Hama Rikyu Garden (see Tsukiji map), where generations of Tokugawa shoguns would retreat to relax from the rigors of feudal duties.

TOP, CENTER: A wooden *taiko* drum for festival use, Miyamoto Unosuke Shoten.

TOP RIGHT: Cow hide tightly stretched over a lacquered wooden frame being fastened by rivets, Miyamoto Unosuke Shoten workshop.

MIDDLE: Drum frames being shaved carefully by carpenters, Miyamoto Unosuke Shoten workshop.

BOTTOM: A personalized set of planes, with the carpenter's name printed on each, Miyamoto Unosuke Shoten workshop.

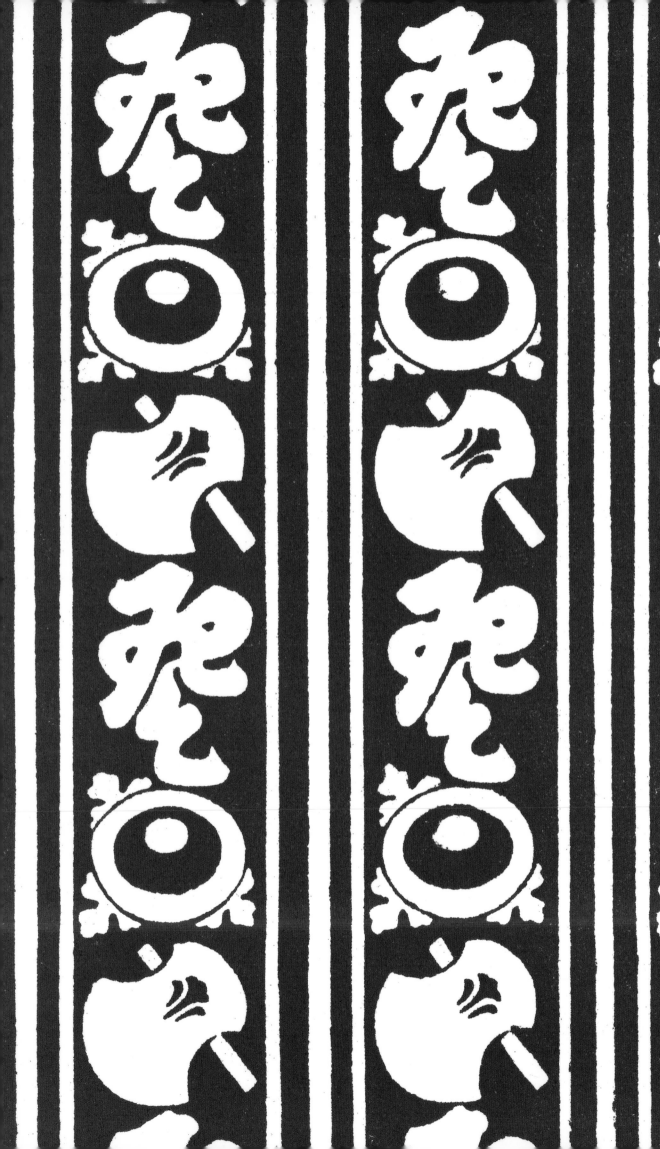

Yanaka & Nezu

Strolling through a Traditional Tokyo Neighborhood

谷中 根津

THEN

Anyone for walking through a captivating maze in the middle of Tokyo? Try this walk in Yanaka. A step away from busy Shinobazu-dori, you will find wonderful neighborhoods with old houses, a miscellany of small shops, large temples, and small roadside shrines—a fascinating mosaic of scenery and everyday life.

Yanaka, an old temple town just north of Ueno, originally was a rice-farming valley on the Aisome River skirting the Ueno Upland. In the 1630s, when the great Kanei-ji temple was built on the hill under the auspices of the second shogun, Hidetada, Yanaka in the temple's rear was designated for a dense cluster of Buddhist temples forming a makeshift defense line to protect the inner city.

During the 1868 Meiji Restoration, when the shogunate fell to the emperor's supporters and modernization, a civil war destroyed the shogun's sanctuary, and the site became what is now Ueno Park, where Japan's first official art academy opened. Artists and students flocking to Ueno to try their talents were happy to find reasonably priced housing in sparsely populated Yanaka, often renting small homes provided by temples. Over the years, the relationships between the landlords and tenants have become so mutually intertwined and intricate that even the greediest developers would rather not touch Yanaka, thus sparing it from Tokyo's avid redevelopment. One of the few areas also to escape destruction by the 1923 earthquake and World War II air raids, Yanaka is now a favorite destination of walkers wishing to enjoy leisurely strolls.

LEFT: Detail of a *chiyogami* paper conceived in a bold Edo-style design and printed with woodblocks, Isetatsu. The three elements—a hatchet, the character for *koto* (a traditional instrument), and a chrysanthemum flower—can be read as "*yoki-koto-kiku*," a play on words that means "I hear (listen to) good things (only), no bad things."

RIGHT: Cats and potted plants add to the cozy neighborhood ambiance of the Yanaka landscape.

YANAKA & NEZU 谷中–根津

NEAREST STATION   Nezu 根津 on the Chiyoda Subway Line 千代田線

ROUTE   Gyokurin-ji temple 玉林寺 ➡ alley walk ➡ crossroads with Himalayan cedar ➡ Allan West studio ➡ Japan Fine Arts Academy 日本美術院 ➡ Zuirin-ji temple 瑞輪寺 ➡ Saiko-ji temple 西光寺 ➡ alley walk ➡ Shisen Kobo incense shop 詩仙香房 ➡ Akatsuka Bekkoten tortoise shell crafts 赤塚鼈甲店 ➡ Space Oguraya gallery スペース小倉屋 ➡ old temple wall ➡ Asakura Sculpture Museum 朝倉彫塑館 ➡ Kyo'o-ji temple 経王寺 ➡ Nakanoya condiments 中野屋 ➡ Midoriya bamboo basket shop 翠屋 ➡ Yanaka Ginza shopping street 谷中銀座 ➡ Snake Road へび道 ➡ Noike sushi restaurant 乃池 ➡ Isetatsu paper shop いせ辰 ➡ Chojiya kimono shop 丁字屋 ➡ Nezu-jinja shrine 根津神社 ➡ Nezu Station 根津駅

ESTIMATED TIME   70 minutes

ESTIMATED DISTANCE   3 miles • 5 kilometers

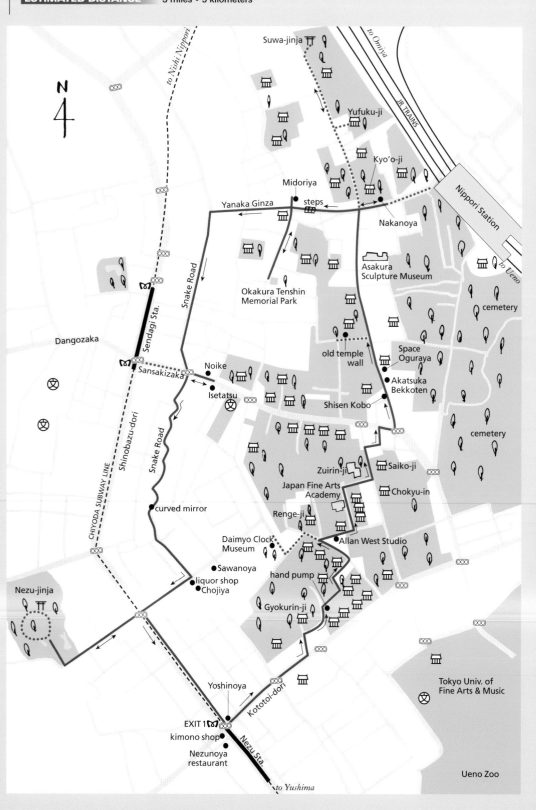

NOW

We start at Nezu Station on the Chiyoda Line for a walk that takes us full circle, returning to the same station. Depending on your time and energy, you can detour to make additional discoveries or exit the loop early to shorten the walk. The route takes you past many beautiful small temples that are well worth adding a few minutes to your walk.

At Nezu Station, use Exit 1 and cross Shinobazu-dori toward the Yoshinoya restaurant to walk on Kototoi-dori. Past several small blocks, look left for a pair of stone lanterns near the second traffic light, marking the entrance to Gyokurin-ji temple. Enter through the temple's metal fence gate, but instead of going to the main hall, take the small cement path to the right.

LEFT: Hydrangea in bloom at Chokyu-in temple.

RIGHT: A bas-relief of a Buddhist deity adorned with cascading spiraea flowers.

The narrow pass along the high temple wall feels like a secret passage. As you walk under huge, daunting old trees, soaring sentinels watching from above, you feel as if you have just opened a doorway into the romantic Tokyo of old. Small houses are quietly packed around the temple wall to its rear. Please remember to proceed quietly through the narrow passageways near homes so as not to disturb the residents. Following the shaded path, look right toward some stone steps to see a delightful, old-fashioned well with a hand pump sheltered under a roof. Communal wells like this were an indispensable part of everyday life in densely populated Edo towns and prewar Tokyo—most have now disappeared.

ABOVE: Lotus with pink buds set to bloom, Renge-ji temple.

RIGHT: Yanaka's narrow lanes, with their ubiquitous potted plants, are a children's haven.

Ascend the steps and follow the path winding left and right. At a T-junction, go left to a crossing dominated by a large Himalayan cedar, then turn right around the tree. Walk straight, passing by Allan West's studio, where you might see the well-known artist at work. A Carnegie-Mellon University art student in oil painting, West first visited Japan in 1982 and fell in love with the traditional methods of decorative Japanese painting. Revisiting, he studied at the Tokyo University of Fine Arts and Music in Ueno Park and now lives happily here with his Japanese wife and children, enjoying his friendly neighbors and the local lifestyle.

Continuing ahead, take the first left onto the broad approach to stately Zuirin-ji temple. Note a splendid modern Japanese building on the left, the Nihon Bijutsu-in (Japan Fine Arts Academy), founded by Okakura Kakuzo (1862–1913), a philosopher and art critic better known by his pen name, Okakura Tenshin. First established in 1898 elsewhere in Yanaka, the academy was relocated here by Yokoyama Taikan (1868–1958), a master painter and Tenshin's most devoted follower. The architectural design of the white-walled academy, rebuilt in 2001, evokes the traditional *kura* warehouse and affirms Tenshin's philosophy of interpreting native cultural heritages in a modern context.

Turning right in front of Zuirin-ji, go left at the T-junction, glancing at a three-story cubic house of concrete enhanced by rather bold wooden slats used for the front door—another example of the

TOP LEFT: An intriguing pathway through a quiet Yanaka neighborhood.

BOTTOM LEFT: Local cats, while not official property owners in Yanaka, are members of the community and roam freely.

THIS PAGE, CLOCKWISE FROM LEFT: A nude statue, a controversial piece of art in an early 20th-century Japan just emerging from feudalism, Asakura Chosokan sculpture museum; museum entrance; museum guest room.

merging of traditional and modern. Next to it is Saiko-ji temple with many quaint stone statues in the small garden.

A short distance ahead, notice a right-hand lane leading to old-fashioned wooden houses with many potted plants beautifying the doorsteps. The lane bends left past more houses. Little shrines nestle in the shade of larger buildings, the enshrined statues almost buried among daily offerings of fresh flowers and water. As you emerge on the sunnier Sansakizaka street and look back after a few steps, the narrow opening you have just come through might now be impossible to see, concealing the charming, hidden neighborhood you have just passed through.

Cross over at the nearby traffic light and walk straight, where you will find many small shops along the way. You will notice, for example, a tofu shop immediately on your left and a lovely incense shop, Shisen Kobo, several buildings ahead, as well as Akatsuka Bekkoten on the right with a window displaying handcrafted items made of tortoise shell. Beyond Akatsuka, you will notice a black-walled house. This is Space Oguraya, a former pawnshop turned art gallery. The house's front section was built in the late 19th century, and the *kura* warehouse on the left, though small and covered by corrugated tin sheets, is a now rare three-story wooden building. Visitors are welcome to walk in and look around when it is open for exhibitions. (Open 10:00–17:00; closed Mondays and Tuesdays, as well as unspecified holidays.)

Farther ahead on the left is a lane between two temples, where a stretch of old wall remains, made of roof tiles piled and plastered together, evoking more poetic times.

Continuing on, you will arrive at Asakura Choso (Sculpture) Museum, formerly the live-in studio of Asakura Fumio (1883–1964), an academic sculptor in post–Meiji Restoration Japan. Like many other Japanese artists at the turn of the 20th century, Asakura strove to learn Western ideals and techniques while maintaining traditional Eastern moral values. Affirming his vision, the building fuses the

TOP LEFT: Show window of Isetatsu paper store.

TOP RIGHT: Chojiya kimono shop.

BOTTOM: Papier mache toy dog, Isetatsu.

RIGHT: Akira Buseki working the edge of an intricately woven flower basket.

FAR RIGHT: Fine bamboo basketry for everyday use at Midoriya.

modern concrete studio and the traditional *sukiya-zukuri*-style private quarters, laid out around a stunning "water garden" with an arrangement of five large rocks embodying the five Confucian virtues. During his sixty years here, the artist found great solace in observing the gushing outflow of natural spring water in the garden and piping it into the kitchen for household use. As you take a self-guided house tour, imagine the artist's daily trips between the two different philosophical realms and his personal struggle to weave together Western knowledge and technology with the native cultural heritage of Japan. (Open 9:30–16:30; closed Mondays and Fridays, as well as government holidays from December 29 to January 3. Tel: 3821–4549.)

Leaving the museum, turn right to reach a crossroads. If you wish to end your walk here, JR Nippori Station is to the right. To continue, cross the road toward the black wooden doors of Kyo'o-ji temple. To the temple's right, Nakanoya is a nostalgic shop selling *tsukudani*—small fish and vegetables boiled in soy sauce and eaten as condiments with steamed rice. More shops line the street toward the station.

Returning to the crossroads, go straight to descend a stairway leading to a lively shopping street, Yanaka Ginza. Just before its entrance, Midoriya to the right is a lovely bamboo basket shop operated by the Buseki family with expert basketry skills. Akira, the third-generation artist, is a frequent winner in annual contemporary arts and crafts exhibitions. Expensive items use now-rare aged bamboo from the roofs of traditional farmhouses. The bamboo has acquired a lovely

amber hue from decades of smoke constantly rising from the fire pit. As even in remote regions old farmhouses have mostly disappeared, smoked bamboo is very precious.

Back at the entrance to Yanaka Ginza, you can take another short detour straight ahead to see Okakura Tenshin Memorial Park, commemorating the Japan Fine Arts Academy's original site. The small park's hexagonal shrine houses a bust of Okakura clad in the academy's Nara period–style (710–94) uniform. Descended from a samurai in the silk business in Yokohama, Okakura studied under Earnest F. Fenollosa (1853–1908), an American philosophy professor who taught at what is now Tokyo University in the 1870s and '80s. In the sweeping trends toward Westernization in the early Meiji period (1868–1912), Okakura and Fenollosa together championed traditional Japanese arts, particularly painting. They strove to have their ideals adopted by the official art academy in Ueno, but conflicting opinions prompted Okakura to found his own private institute here with support from many devoted followers. Among his students who later attained eminence are Yokoyama Taikan, Shimomura Kanzan, and Hishida Shunso. In 1905, Okakura was invited by the Boston Museum of Fine Arts to serve as the Chinese and Japanese Department's assistant curator. He spent his later years traveling frequently between Tokyo and Boston.

Finally walking into Yanaka Ginza, enjoy browsing around diverse shops offering just about everything to meet the everyday needs of local customers. At the end of the linear market, turn left to follow a gently curving road, which actually traces the Aisome River, now routed underground to Shinobazu Pond. Until the Shinobazu-dori highway was laid in 1895 on the river's west bank, this meandering

TOP: Nezu-jinja shrouded in silence on a hazy spring evening.
BOTTOM: Central gate of Nezu-jinja, turn of the 18th century.
RIGHT: A long tunnel of red *torii* gates to an Inari shrine, Nezu-jinja.

way, locally known as Hebi-michi (Snake Road), was Yanaka's main thoroughfare.

The road intersects with Sansakizaka at a traffic light. A right turn at this crossing will take you to Sendagi Station on the Chiyoda Line; a left turn will take you to Noike sushi restaurant on the left and Isetatsu paper shop on the right. Noike is famous for its *anago-zushi* with delicately cooked conger. (Open 11:30–20:00; closed on Wednesdays.) Isetatsu specializes in irresistibly beautiful, hand-printed Edo *chiyogami* (Japanese decorated paper) and other products—ideal for gifts.

Back at the traffic light, continue along the curvy road for several minutes. Keep right when another road from the left connects at a 45-degree angle with the road. Not long after this junction, the road curves left and intersects with a relatively large street with a liquor store ahead on the right-hand corner. Pausing to look left, notice Sawanoya, a family-operated inn popular among international travelers (Tel: 3822–2251). Beyond the liquor store, in a handsome wooden building, is a kimono shop called Chojiya, in business since 1895. Originally a dyer who rinsed dyed fabric in the Aisome River at the shop front, Chojiya now serves its longtime customers with the cleaning and re-tailoring of delicate silk kimonos and sells various small items made of dyed silk and cotton.

Turning right in front of the liquor shop, return to Shinobazu-dori—Nezu Station is to the left. Time permitting, visit Nezu-jinja a few small blocks straight ahead, marked by a large *torii* gate. The luxuriously crafted shrine was built in 1706 by the fifth shogun, Tokugawa Tsunayoshi, to celebrate the adoption of his nephew as heir to the throne. In late spring, brilliant azalea blooms embellish the shrine's hillside. A tunnel of small *torii* gates leading to a secondary shrine is an enjoyable detour. The azalea festival from mid-April to the first week of May is a lively affair with many stalls selling food, antiques, and such. The main shrine opens to visitors for viewing the usually off-limits interior at 12 NOON and 14:00. Follow the map to return to Nezu Station.

TOP: Ornately decorated roof of Nezu-jinja main hall.
BOTTOM: A stone fox guarding the Inari shirne, Nezu-jinja.

Index

Acknowledgments

The publisher wishes to express its gratitude to the following shops and organizations for generously granting permission to reproduce some of the photographs in this volume:

Asakura Chosokan   PAGE 73 (ALL)

Atago-jinja   PAGES 50–52

Bunsendo   PAGE 58 (TOP)

Fukagawa Edo Shiryokan   PAGE 35

Isetatsu   PAGES 66 AND 74 (TOP LEFT AND BOTTOM)

Ishida Biwaten   PAGES 48 (BOTTOM) AND 49

Japan Actors' Association   PAGES 44 (TOP) AND 45; PHOTOS BY Iwata Akira

Kawasaki   PAGE 28 (BOTTOM)

Maekawa   PAGE 64 (BOTTOM)

Midoriya   PAGE 75 (BOTH)

Miyamoto Unosuke Shoten   PAGES 64 (TOP RIGHT) AND 65 (ALL)

Nihon Token   PAGE 46

Ozu Washi   PAGES 16 (TOP) AND 17 (BOTTOM RIGHT)

Sushi Tsukasa   PAGE 43 (TOP)

Tofuya Ukai   JACKET

Toranomon Sunaba   PAGE 48 (TOP, BOTH)

Wholesale Co-operative of Tokyo Fish Market   PAGES 39–42

Yubendo   PAGES 16 (BOTTOM) AND 17 (TOP LEFT AND RIGHT)

Photo Credits

Additional photographs were shot and/or provided by the following:

Inoue Akira   PAGE 22

Iwata Akira   PAGE 44 (TOP) AND 45 (BOTTOM)

National Diet Library   PAGE 38

National Museum of Japanese History   PAGES 11 (TOP) AND 14

Nihon Sumo Kyokai   PAGE 26

Ozawa Hiroyuki   PAGES 30 AND 32 (TOP)

Sato Motonobu (Seven Photo)   PAGE 23

Tofuya Ukai   PAGE 53 (BOTH)

Tohoku University Library   PAGES 5, 34 (TOP), AND ENDPAPERS

Yoshitoku   PAGE 25 (RIGHT)

(英文版) 東京ウォークス
Tokyo: Exploring the City of the Shogun

2007年2月26日　第1刷発行

著　者　圓佛須美子
写　真　中里和人
発行者　富田 充
発行所　講談社インターナショナル株式会社
　　　　〒112-8652 東京都文京区音羽 1-17-14
　　　　電話　03-3944-6493 (編集部)
　　　　　　　03-3944-6492 (マーケティング部・業務部)
　　　　ホームページ　www.kodansha-intl.com

印刷・製本所　大日本印刷株式会社

落丁本・乱丁本は購入書店名を明記のうえ、講談社インターナショナル業務部宛
にお送りください。送料小社負担でお取替えいたします。なお、この本について
のお問い合わせは、編集部宛にお願いいたします。本書の無断複写 (コピー)
は著作権法の例外を除き、禁じられています。

定価はカバーに表示してあります。

© 圓佛須美子 2007
Printed in Japan
ISBN 978-4-7700-3033-7

TOKYO
WALKING AREAS

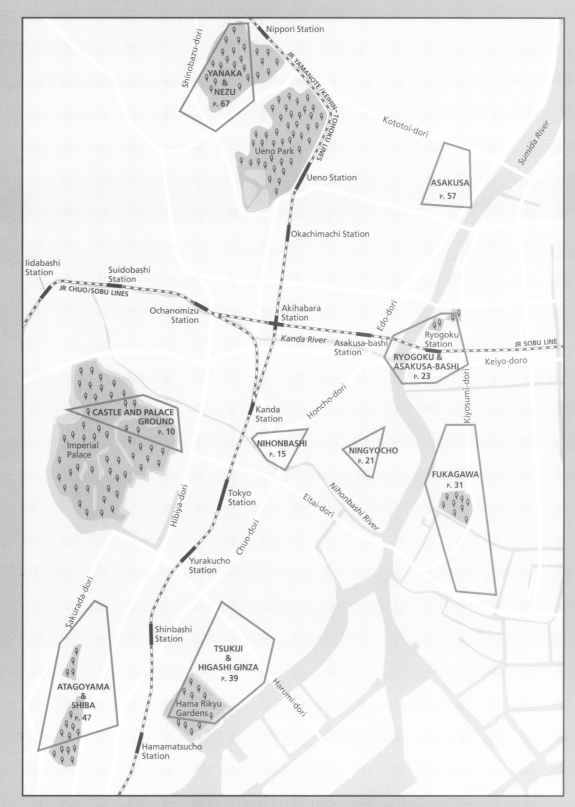

YANAKA & NEZU P. 67

Nippori Station

Shinobazu-dori

JR YAMANOTE /KEIHIN-TOHOKU LINES

Kototoi-dori

Sumida River

Ueno Park

ASAKUSA P. 57

Ueno Station

Okachimachi Station

Iidabashi Station

Suidobashi Station

JR CHUO/SOBU LINES

Ochanomizu Station

Akihabara Station

Edo-dori

Ryogoku Station

JR SOBU LINE

Kanda River

Asakusa-bashi Station

Keiyo-doro

RYOGOKU & ASAKUSA-BASHI P. 23

CASTLE AND PALACE GROUND P. 10

Kanda Station

Honcho-dori

Kiyosumi-dori

Imperial Palace

NIHONBASHI P. 15

NINGYOCHO P. 21

FUKAGAWA P. 31

Hibiya-dori

Tokyo Station

Nihonbashi River

Eitai-dori

Yurakucho Station

Sakurada-dori

Shinbashi Station

TSUKIJI & HIGASHI GINZA P. 39

ATAGOYAMA & SHIBA P. 47

Hama Rikyu Gardens

Harumi-dori

Chuo-dori

Hamamatsucho Station